Power Up!

GRIDIRON

EDITION

EDITION

Devotional
Thoughts for
FOOTBALL
FANS

DAVE BRANON, EDITOR

DISCOVERY HOUSE
PUBLISHERS®

Feeding the Soul with the Word of God

Power Up! Gridiron Edition
©2011 by Discovery House Publishers
All rights reserved.

Discovery House Publishers is affiliated with RBC Ministries,
Grand Rapids, Michigan.

Discovery House books are distributed to the trade exclusively by
Barbour Publishing, Inc., Uhrichsville, Ohio.

Interior design by Sherri L. Hoffman
Cover design by Steve Gier

ISBN: 978-1-57293-456-6

Printed in the United States of America
11 12 13 14 / 10 9 8 7 6 5 4 3 2 1

CONTENTS

INTRODUCTION

American football fans have a long-standing love affair with their gridiron sport.

On weekends in the fall, the romance begins with Friday night lights as masses of people gather in a vast variety of football fields in small towns and big cities across the land to play, cheer for, and watch high school football. In an average year, more than 1,100,000 young men suit up and play this great game in front of their fellow students, their teachers, their parents, and interested fans of their school. More than 14,000 high schools in the USA field football teams.

On Saturdays, the affection between fans and football cranks up a few notches as people turn their attention to the college gridiron. There the excitement turns into frenzy as schools as small as Maranatha Baptist Bible College (900 students) and as large as the Ohio State University (50,000 students) field teams that bring pride and honor to their schools. With major college football teams, the fan base often grows to a nationwide audience of avid followers—and millions gather in front of their wide-screens to marvel at the athleticism and strength of their undergraduate gridiron favorites.

One indicator of college football's popularity is the size of the stadiums that host its games. In Ann Arbor, Michigan, the University of Michigan Wolverines play in a structure that can officially seat 109,901 fans but that has held more than 111,000 football fans. Close behind are Penn State's Beaver Stadium (107,282), Neyland Stadium at the University of Tennessee (104,079), and the Ohio State Buckeyes' 101,568-seat Ohio Stadium.

For months, football conversation dominates Twitter messages, blogs, and watercooler and lunchroom discussions. Who hasn't been met in the church foyer on Sunday with a handshake and a "Did you see the game yesterday?"

And then, of course, there is Sunday and the National Football League—the juggernaut of all sports entities in North America. No other sport touches the NFL in popularity from sea to shining sea. This league dominates the all-time rankings of television shows ever broadcast or cablecast in the US. The 2010 Super Bowl, for instance, became the highest rated TV program in the history of ratings—knocking the 1983 finale of M*A*S*H off its perch. Of the Top 10–rated programs of all time, five are Super Bowl games.

According to surveys, pro football far outdistances its rival sports leagues—the NBA, Major League Baseball, and all others—in fan appreciation. A Harris Poll has been taken on this subject every year for decades, and since 1965, pro football has been the top choice of sports fans. In a recent survey, the NFL was the favorite sport of 31 percent of Americans with baseball far behind in second at 16 percent.

So there it is—an incontrovertible fact: Football reigns supreme in the American sports world.

But what is it that draws so many people to this sport?

Football is a circus-like spectacle. It's a once-a-week event, meaning that each contest has a built-up demand and a built-in "wait for it" factor. It's a destination event—with people coming early for tailgate parties and other socializing events. It's an entertainment package—complete with marching bands and cheerleaders and all kinds of crazy fans dressed in outlandish ways. It's a battle—a manly mini-war played out for all to see on a symmetrically designed theater of conflict. Warlike in its nature as teams defend their land and try to prevent the advancement of the enemy through physically demanding tactics, it is gladiatorial without the nasty outcome. And it's a display of athleticism of various sorts. Strong men pounding each other. Fast men outracing each other. Multitalented men throwing passes or catching them. Smaller men kicking the ball either to others or through uprights.

As we enjoy football, we can't help but learn lessons about life and competition and success and pain and joy. And if we look a little deeper, we can even see illustrations that can point to truths that are more long-lasting than any Super Bowl trophy or NCAA BCS title.

In *Power Up! Gridiron Edition*, we've tried to put your love for football together with your interest in spiritual things in order to help you grow in your faith in and knowledge of Jesus Christ. We are football fans too, and we think the wisdom of the Bible has so much to say to us about what is really important in life.

Football. It dominates the sports scene in the fall—and for much of the rest of the year. But because nothing should dominate our lives as much as our love for God through Jesus Christ, we focus in this book on Him and how to live as He wants us to. And we hope that helps make you a winner.

DAVE BRANON, EDITOR
Power Up! Gridiron Edition

THE TOP 100 CHRISTIAN
FOOTBALL PLAYERS

One of the bonus features we thought you would enjoy as you look through this gridiron edition of our Power Up! *devotional series is a list of the Top 100 Christian football players of all time. At the end of each article, you'll find a short note about one of the men we think belongs in the Top 100. This is our second such list—the first was in* Power Up! Diamond Edition. *If you haven't seen that one, pick up a copy and see what you think about our list of Top 100 Christian baseball players.*

Compiling this list is former Sports Spectrum *magazine and radio associate Rob Bentz, who spent several years working as an integral part of the magazine staff. During his years at SS, one of Rob's tasks was preparing a weekly NFL predictions piece for our website sports report called "The Daily." He showed his knowledge of the NFL with his excellent prognostications—often out-guessing the experts even at the network known as the worldwide leader.*

Now a pastor in Colorado, Rob hasn't lost his interest in sports or his adept touch at making picks. This time, though, his picks deal with the Top 100, which he explains below.

I like football. And I like ice cream.

Putting together a list of the Top 100 Christ-following football stars is similar to tackling the task of choosing your favorite ice cream. Oh, it's fun! But you test and evaluate and consider . . . then you realize they're *all* good. It's really hard to come to any sort of definitive decision.

It's tough!

Yet for the purpose of this devotional book, we had to become a coach of sorts and make some tough decisions. Who made the team? Who got cut? Before we reveal the results of our top gridiron choices, let's examine the decision-making process.

First, we had to determine who is a Christian football star. Who on this side of heaven can really know the true heart of a man? Can we determine definitively those who are truly born-again, as opposed to those who are not? Can any of us know for sure that another person has trusted in Jesus Christ as his Savior? It's a difficult task for someone who's been affected by Adam's sin to make a judgment call on another human being who has also been affected by the fall.

Because we cannot be in every locker room, talk to every NFL player, or interview the athletes up for consideration, we have to depend on other players, coaches, assistant coaches, broadcasters, journalists, team chaplains, and sports ministry leaders to give us insight into the lives of the believers who waged war on NFL turf every Sunday. In the end, we believe that we have wisely chosen the best Christian football players at their respective positions. Yet, we likely missed a few committed Christ-followers who would have been worthy of being honored in such a list.

Second, we were forced to choose between on-field performance and the impact of the athlete's Christian testimony and ministry that transcends the game. We opted for an unscientific combination of both—leaning more heavily on performance. For example, we chose to rate the impressive passing numbers and longevity of former Jacksonville Jaguars star signal caller Mark Brunell ahead of Buffalo Bills legendary back-up quarterback Frank Reich and the boldness he displayed professing Christ to the media following his leading the Bills to their historic come-from-behind victory over the Houston Oilers in the 1993 AFC Wild-Card Game. Frank is an incredibly articulate, knowledgeable, humble man of God, yet his career performance cannot compare to that of Brunell's.

Third, through many years of covering sports for *Sports Spectrum* magazine and *Sports Spectrum* radio, we have interacted with and observed many Christian athletes. We recognize that none of the men we have featured then, or in this Top 100 now, are perfect. They have their faults. A few have made some poor life decisions. Yet in spite of their failures, they remain under God's amazing grace. They remain men striving to honor Him with their lives. So, we have chosen one player, Eugene Robinson, whose sin was made very public, yet he has been restored.

This reminds us that any time a Christian athlete is featured in this way—as a magazine such as *Sports Spectrum* has done for many years—we risk being embarrassed should one of the athletes stumble spiritually. Putting these guys in a book even further establishes their stories and provides greater opportunity for scorn should they stumble out of fellowship with God.

Fourth, we tried very hard to allow statistical and empirical evidence to dictate who made the cut—and who did not—in spite of personal preference. (Statistics for active players are current through the 2009 season.) For example, it was tough to develop the list and not include some of my favorite Christian athletes and coaches from my 15 years in covering sports for *Sports Spectrum*.

Napoleon Kaufman was one of the nicest, most humble, and gracious athletes I ever interviewed. But his NFL success was relatively short, because he sensed God's call to pastoral ministry. Kaufman left the NFL at the age of 27, and he has now become a teaching pastor in California with a thriving ministry. Napoleon is a great guy. But his playing career didn't give him the longevity needed to make the Top 100.

I work alongside former NFL tight end Rich Griffith in pastoral ministry in Colorado. Rich's career spanned eight years and two NFL teams. Yet statistically, he didn't catch enough passes or score enough touchdowns to make the cut. (It's tough to tell a friend and partner in ministry that he didn't make the cut—but that's what I had to do.)

Fifth, we attempted to honor the many diverse talents and abilities represented in the game of football. Whether it was the size and strength of line play, the speed and agility of a running back or wide receiver, or the unique kicking ability of a placekicker, we sought to highlight the best at each key position on the field. So among the Top 100 you will find both the size and intensity of defensive end Reggie White and the skill and precision of kicker Jason Elam.

So it is on these criteria that we humbly present our Top 100 Christian Football Players on the pages of this devotional book.

We believe that formulating a Top 100 is a worthwhile effort because it is one way to honor men who've enjoyed outstanding football careers and yet placed a high value on living out their Christian faith in a tough, violent, and intense sport that often does not look fondly upon followers of Jesus Christ.

As a fellow football fan, I hope you will enjoy reading the names listed as the Top 100 Christian Football Players and the brief stories behind their inclusion.

Yet more important than enjoying the list we've compiled, it is my prayer that you will be inspired and challenged by the biblical truths presented on the following pages.

—ROB BENTZ
Colorado Springs, Colorado

1. QUIET, BUT NOT SILENT

Scrimmage Line:
Developing a passion for Jesus

"We proclaim to you the eternal life, which was with the Father and has appeared to us."

1 JOHN 1:2

Tony Dungy is a winner. He proved that to the football world back in 2007 when he led the Indianapolis Colts to victory in Super Bowl XLI. But that's not what makes him a winner in many people's eyes. It's not his football accomplishments but his faith and character that define this man.

Shortly after winning the Super Bowl, Dungy released an autobiography titled *Quiet Strength*. The title fits Tony, but there is one thing not so quiet about him—his desire to let others know about Jesus. "People look at me and see a calm, cool guy on the sidelines. I want them to know that my Christian faith affects my coaching and everything I do." The book rose to No. 1 on the *New York Times* bestseller list.

FAST FACT:
Tony Dungy played defensive back for the Pittsburgh Steelers when they beat the Dallas Cowboys 35-31 in Super Bowl XIII on January 21, 1979.

Indeed, Tony Dungy is quiet by nature. But he is *not* silent about his faith!

The apostle John was like that. He too was willing to get "loud" about being a believer in Jesus. He wrote to the early Christian church: "The life appeared; we have seen it and *testify* to it, and we *proclaim* to you the eternal life, which was with the Father and has appeared to us" (1 John 1:2, emphasis added).

The two italicized words above mean "to be a witness" and

"to make known openly." John was not silent about his faith, and he wanted other believers to be all about proclaiming and testifying too.

The reason? He knew and loved Jesus. He had heard, seen, and even touched Him.

This passion for Jesus is reflected in the life of Tony Dungy—though he has seen Jesus through the eyes of faith alone (2 Corinthians 5:7). What about you? Are you proclaiming Jesus in your words and actions? It's okay to be quiet, just don't be silent about your faith.

—TOM FELTEN

POINT AFTER

As you talk with friends or neighbors today, make it a point to tell them about a Scripture passage or an experience with God that has spoken to your heart recently. Don't be silent—consciously consider how you might "proclaim" your love for Jesus to them.

From the Playbook: Read 1 John 1:1–7.

NFL Quarterbacks

NO. 1. ROGER STAUBACH College: 1963, Heisman Trophy; Pro: 1969–1979 Dallas; 1971, Super Bowl MVP; 6 Pro Bowls; 1978, NFL Man of the Year; 1985, Inducted into Hall of Fame; 22,700 passing yards, 153 TDs.

FAITH QUOTE: *"God put it all together in His infinite wisdom by sending His Son here. I believe that Jesus Christ was the Son of God who died for our sins and came back from the dead."*

2. STAND BY YOUR TEAM

Scrimmage Line:
Following God with zeal

"As long as [Josiah] lived, [the Israelites] did not fail to follow the Lord, the God of their fathers."

2 CHRONICLES 34:33

It doesn't really matter when the season begins or ends—whenever you have a University of Michigan fan and an Ohio State Buckeye fan in the same room, there will always be banter. Someone will always raise his or her banner with pride!

What is it about college football that ignites this deep passion in people? Texas vs. Oklahoma. Florida vs. Georgia. USC vs. Notre Dame. Oregon vs. Oregon State. Alabama vs. Auburn. Army vs. Navy. Why do people have such zealous loyalty for their teams in these monumental clashes?

FAST FACT:

The Oklahoma-Texas showdown is called The Red River Shootout. Unlike most college football rivalries, it is played on a neutral field.

The appeal of college football is rooted in the simple notion that your team represents you, your state, your alma mater, and your youth. It has a magical ability to reconnect you to your past. Steeped in silly traditions, favorite chants and cheers, and good old-fashioned archrivals, college football has a way of bringing people back to their roots.

Judah's King Josiah could do that too. He had a unique ability to reconnect people to their past. His zeal for following God's precepts marked him as Judah's most obedient king. The book of 2 Kings records his heroic efforts to reform the people of Judah by reminding them of their sin and by boldly cutting down the idols they were serving. Josiah's leadership represented his great-grandfather, Hezekiah, who had created a tradition among the people of godliness and honor.

What is it inside of you that ignites your passion? What things in your life and in your personal history seem worth fighting for? I hope it is more than football.

It was said of King Josiah, "Neither before nor after Josiah was there a king like him who turned to the LORD as he did—with all his heart and with all his soul and with all his strength" (2 Kings 23:25). Could that be said of you?

—MOLLY RAMSEYER

POINT AFTER

Ask God today if there are "idols" in your life that need to be smashed. What captures your passion? Does God appear in your Top 5?

From the Playbook: Read 2 Kings 23.

TOP 100 NFL Quarterbacks

NO. 2. BART STARR 1956–1971 Green Bay; 1966, NFL MVP; 1967, 1968, Super Bowl MVP; 1977, Inducted into HOF; 24,718 passing yards, 152 TDs.

FAITH QUOTE: *"If your life is truly prioritized—if you put God first, you put your family second, and anything else third—you have very few problems."*

3. TAKING CHANCES

Scrimmage Line:
Stepping out on faith

*"Therefore go and make disciples of all nations,
baptizing them in the name of the Father and
of the Son and of the Holy Spirit."*

MATTHEW 28:19

Were you as surprised as I was when the New Orleans Saints attempted an onside kick to start the second half of Super Bowl XLIV? Head coach Sean Payton showed a lot of moxie with that call.

Had it gone wrong for the Saints, the Indianapolis Colts would have had to go about 40 yards behind Peyton Manning to get a touchdown and secure a 17-6 lead. Momentum would have been in their favor, and the party may well have been over.

FAST FACT:

Another famous onside kick took place in Super Bowl XXX when Bill Cowher's Pittsburgh Steelers got the ball back that way while trailing 20-10.

What did it take for Coach Payton to stick his neck out like that? It took a lot of faith, that's what. He trusted his players. He trusted his preparation. And he trusted his own judgment. While the second-guessers and analysts might have wondered why he was doing this, in his estimation, he wasn't doing anything foolhardy.

Do we ever surprise anyone with an act of faith? Do we ever stick our necks out for the gospel of the Lord Jesus Christ—knowing that what we are attempting just might not work and we might end up being ridiculed if it doesn't?

For instance, it takes courage and a bit of moxie to approach someone we know and ask him or her about faith in Jesus Christ. It's a little like an onside kick in a surprising situation, because if the other person doesn't respond as we would like, we may feel as if we have failed. But there is a difference. When we take a chance in football—the results are up to us completely. But when we step out on faith as a Christian, the results are in God's hands. He asks us to take the bold action of witnessing for Him, and He promises to give us the results He wants.

—DAVE BRANON

POINT AFTER

Write down the names of three people with whom you would like to share the gospel. What would be the best way to present the gospel to these people?

From the Playbook: Read Acts 8:26–40.

NFL Quarterbacks

NO. 3. TERRY BRADSHAW 1970–1983 Pittsburgh; 1978, NFL MVP; 1979, Super Bowl MVP; 1989, Inducted into HOF; 27,989 passing yards, 212 TDs.

FAITH QUOTE: *"One of the things I've done since I got saved . . . is not necessarily make excuses for myself anymore. My preachers helped me tremendously with that. I know God loves me. I know He forgives me."*

4. BELIEVE IT . . . YOU WERE CHOSEN

"You did not choose me, but I chose you and appointed you to go and bear fruit."

JOHN 15:16

I was watching the pro football draft with an NFL player, and he shared with me that the time he was drafted had been such an incredible moment. As he talked about that special day, he turned to me and said, "It felt good to be picked."

Getting picked to enter the National Football League is certainly a huge honor, but it is nothing compared with what John 15:16 tells us about.

In that verse we learn that Jesus picked John to represent Him. By extension, He also chooses all of us who put our faith in Him. The fact that He chose you is absolutely awesome. There may have been times when you were overlooked in life, but know this: Jesus chose you.

Jesus uses fruit as an example to describe and illustrate His point. Fruit is a great visual example, because the nature of fruit is to bear more fruit. I believe that when Jesus selected His disciples, He had a specific purpose for each one. But along with His selection, He also

FAST FACT:
The first NFL draft was held on February 8, 1936, in Philadelphia. Heisman Trophy winner Jay Berwanger from the University of Chicago was picked by the Philadelphia Eagles and traded to the Chicago Bears. He opted not to play pro football.

assigned them the task of bearing fruit. He knew that it was up to each one of them to carry on His work.

The same truth is still relevant regarding us today. The Lord needs you and me to carry on His work to provide His message to others.

This truth can have a profound effect on your life if you believe He has selected you for this specific time. Thank Jesus for that through this prayer. *Jesus, here I am. Direct my life and place me exactly where you need me to be so I can do the most good for you. My life belongs to you. Amen.*

Jesus chose you to use you. How cool is that!

—ADAM YBARRA

POINT AFTER

Take a step to share the message of God with someone. It will rock your world.

From the Playbook: Read John 15.

NFL Quarterbacks

NO. 4. KURT WARNER 1999–2010 St. Louis Rams, New York Giants, Arizona; 1999, 2001, NFL MVP; 2000, Super Bowl MVP; 2008, NFL Man of the Year; 2009, Bart Starr Award; 4 Pro Bowls; 32,344 passing yards, 208 TDs.

FAITH QUOTE: *"Life as a Christian is about living every day for Jesus—in and despite all circumstances."*

5. GREAT EXPECTATIONS

*"I urge you to live a life worthy of
the calling you have received."*

EPHESIANS 4:1

Do your remember the 2007 Fiesta Bowl? Boise State was matched against tradition-rich Oklahoma, and the Broncos weren't exactly a hands-down favorite to beat the mighty Sooners.

Sure, they had won the Western Athletic Conference and were ranked No. 9 in the country, but they were playing a school with seven national championships in its history. It appeared to be a classic David and Goliath matchup.

But when Broncos coach Chris Petersen chose to attempt two trick plays—first a hook-and-ladder that resulted in an overtime-forcing touchdown and then the Statue of Liberty, which capped Boise State's remarkable 43-42 win in the second overtime—the Broncos proved they deserved to be called one of the nation's top college football teams.

As Christians, we have Oklahoma-sized challenges as well. We are called to be set apart from the rest of the world. There's an expectation that because we belong to Jesus, we must do our part. In Ephesians 4, Paul urges Christians to live a life worthy of the calling they have received. He says part of living for Christ

FAST FACT:
Ian Johnson, who scored the game-winning points in the Fiesta Bowl, proposed to his girlfriend, Chrissy Popadics, during a post-game interview. They were married in July 2007.

involves a life of being humble and gentle, patient and loving toward each other (v. 2). Sure, it's a big challenge to live up to—kind of like the obstacle Boise State faced in having to beat a more recognized team in order to be seen as one of the best. And just as the Broncos had to do what their coach asked them to do, if we want to "live a life worthy" of Jesus' calling, we have to do what our Savior and Lord expects of us.

It's a special thing to be part of God's family, so we should honor God's choice by living in a way that is worthy of our Lord.

—JEFF ARNOLD

POINT AFTER

Are you holding up your end of the bargain when it comes to living for Jesus? It's easy to say you're part of God's family, but when it comes down to it, what are you doing to set yourself apart? Ask Jesus to reveal to you ways that you can live for Him more.

From the Playbook: Read Ephesians 4.

NFL Quarterbacks

NO. 5. DREW BREES   2001– San Diego, New Orleans; 2004, NFL Comeback Player of the Year; 2006, NFL Man of the Year; 2008, Offensive Player of the Year; 2006, 2008, Led NFL in passing yards (4,418; 5069); 2010, Super Bowl MVP; 4 Pro Bowls; 30,646 passing yards, 202 TDs.

FAITH QUOTE: *"God puts us in positions, all the time, for a reason. God is doing it to strengthen you."*

6. CALLING AUDIBLES

*"I have hidden your word in my heart that
I might not sin against you."*

PSALM 119:11

When the quarterback breaks the huddle, he comes out with a specific play in mind. But as he looks over the defensive set of the opposition and gets under center, he may realize that the defense already has the play figured out. He will then quickly call out an audible to his offensive line, receivers, and running back. Then, once everyone is on the same page, the quarterback will signal for the hike. The offense hopes his new play will catch the defense off guard.

FAST FACT:

Here's the name of one Tampa Bay play from a few years ago: "West Left Slot, Fox Three Wide, Bingo Z Smash on One." How would you like to memorize about 30 of these?

But where does the quarterback get ideas for these audibles? Certainly he cannot bring the full playbook onto the field, nor does he have enough time to check with his offensive coordinator or even read his wristband play guide. Instead, he must have several different plays memorized so he can call a new play that is best suited for a particular defense.

As Christians, we have a "playbook" given to us by the One who knows all the right plays in every circumstance. No matter which one of Satan's defenses (despair, condemnation, temptation) is thrown our way, we know that we have a loving God who has given us instructions through His Word and promises of His help. God's guidance in the Word never fails, and it actually changes our heart when we continually study and memorize it.

When difficult circumstances or temptations surface in our lives—and in the lives of our friends—we may need to call an audible from God's Word. If we study and memorize God's Word, we'll be ready with the needed change of plan and direction.

Just as a seasoned quarterback applies the playbook with an audible, we too can apply the teachings of the Word to any situation.

—GEOFF HENDERSON

POINT AFTER

Write a Bible verse on a note card. Try to commit one new verse to memory each week by studying it for a few minutes before you go to sleep. In time, these few minutes will lead to a box full of note cards and a better grasp of God's Word.

From the Playbook: Read Psalm 119:9–11. Choose a memory verse from this passage.

TOP 100 NFL Quarterbacks

NO. 6. MARK BRUNELL 1994–2009 Green Bay, Jacksonville, Washington, New Orleans; 3 Pro Bowls; 31,928 passing yards, 182 TDs.

FAITH QUOTE: *"I know my life has meaning because of the love Jesus Christ has shown me."*

7. KICKED AROUND

"In all things God works for the good of those who love him, who have been called according to his purpose."

ROMANS 8:28

Several years ago, the team I was playing for acquired a new head coach. He and I got off to a rough start when I missed some field-goal attempts. I had to remember that God had placed him in authority over me (Hebrews 13:17)—even as he humiliated me in front of my teammates and 68,000 fans.

FAST FACT:

Through the end of the 2009 football season, Matt Stover hadn't missed an extra point for 14 seasons. During that time, he nailed more than 300 extra points without a miss.

Jesus endured the ultimate humiliation before the resurrection, but later He sat at the right hand of the throne of God. His willingness to go to the cross for us should encourage us as we face opposition.

During my struggle, the team brought in another kicker to replace me. I submitted the situation to God and prayed that His will would be served. It's easy to be willing to be used by God during good times, but now I had to be willing to be used through my hard times.

The other kicker was gone after five weeks.

God gave me strength to persevere through the most difficult circumstances of my career (Philippians 4:13). He allowed me to make 18 straight field goals to finish the season and keep my job.

All eyes were on me during this trial, but my eyes were fixed on Christ. I was encouraged as my teammates later told me that an inner peace had shone through me and that my ability to handle my coach with self-control spoke volumes to them. I am confident that God used this incident to further His kingdom.

Are you willing to be used, even if it could cost you your career? Trust that God has it all under control and that He "works for the good of those who love him" (Romans 8:28).

—MATT STOVER

POINT AFTER

List three struggles that you are enduring right now. How can you use each one to bring glory to God?

From the Playbook: Read Hebrews 12:1–3.

TOP 100 NFL Quarterbacks

NO. 7. RANDALL CUNNINGHAM 1985–2001 Philadelphia, Minnesota, Dallas, Baltimore Ravens; 1988, 1990, 1998, NFL Player of the Year; 1992, NFL Comeback Player of the Year; 4 Pro Bowls; 29,979 passing yards, 207 TDs.

FAITH QUOTE: *"Look at Jesus. He was in very nature God but 'did not consider equality with God something to be grasped' [Philippians 2:6]. That's how I feel as a human being. God is my friend. He is my Father. But in no way can I ever think more highly of myself than I ought to because I must be a humble man."*

8. WHO WILL YOU FOLLOW?

Scrimmage Line:
Choosing God's way

*"If the Lord is God, follow him;
but if Baal is God, follow him."*

1 KINGS 18:21

"Hey, Ken," our line coach, Jimmy McNally, said to me one day during my days as an offensive lineman for the Cincinnati Bengals in the 1990s, "Did you work on your pass sets today?"

"Uhh, sure," I replied, even though I knew it wasn't true. Not wanting my coach to see me as anything but the hardest of workers, I chose to lie rather then have him think less of me. Minutes later, while I was still sitting at my locker, God convinced me that I needed to return to Jimmy and apologize for lying. So I trudged up to his room and confessed my sin. He graciously accepted my apology.

FAST FACT:
Ken Moyer played on the offensive line for the Cincinnati Bengals in 71 games from 1989 to 1991 and 1993 to 1994.

So often in life we are faced with a choice: Will we follow God, even when it is inconvenient or costly? In times like those, we would do well to remember Elijah. Surrounded by a community that had chosen disobedience as a way of life, Elijah stood strong and chose to follow God, even if that meant having the king chase him around trying to kill him. And his community responded by turning back to God.

We all face difficult choices: Will I maintain sexual purity from this day forward? Will I cheat just a little on my taxes?

Will I help that person in need? Will I lie to my coach or boss to avoid trouble?

In little choices as well as big, God calls us to follow Him by obeying His commands. Start today. Put a stake in the ground and decide to choose to follow Him regardless. If you blow it in the future, ask for forgiveness and move on.

Jesus simply asks us to resolutely choose God's way. To do anything else invites trouble and distress!

—KEN MOYER

POINT AFTER

What specific struggles am I having? Were they things Ken mentioned? Other things? How can I follow God instead of my sinful desires?

From the Playbook: Read 1 Kings 18:16–39.

NFL Quarterbacks

NO. 8. RICH GANNON 1987–2004 Minnesota, Washington, Kansas City, Oakland; 2002, Led NFL in completions (418) and yards (4,689); 4 Pro Bowls; 2000, 2002, NFL Player of the Year; 2002, NFL MVP; 28,743 passing yards, 189 TDs.

FAITH QUOTE: *"I prayed to the Lord for guidance and strength—that He would take control of my life."*

9. FAITHFUL WITH THE FUNDS

Scrimmage Line:
Handling money wisely

*"Well done, good and faithful servant!
You have been faithful with a few things."*

MATTHEW 25:21

Is it even possible to learn anything about money management from today's highly paid athletes? Most people would say no, but several years ago running back Willis McGahee proved us all wrong.

During the January 2003 Fiesta Bowl, McGahee sustained a knee injury so severe that many thought his football career was over. Fortunately for him, just hours before the game, McGahee had made the wise decision to secure a $2.5 million disability insurance policy. Had the injury been so severe that he never played a down in the NFL, the policy would have helped him make up some of his lost earnings.

Now, you may never receive a $10 million signing bonus as some professional athletes do, and your career is probably not based on your physical health, but the lesson here still applies: It is important to be closely involved in your finances, to plan ahead, and to treat money with great care.

Money is one of the most commonly mentioned subjects in the Bible. Money matters to God. In Matthew 25 Jesus tells a story of three servants who had been entrusted with money (vv. 14–30). Their master expected them to invest that money wisely, not to squander or abuse what had been given to them. To those workers who used their money wisely, the master said, "You have been faithful with a few things; I will put you in charge of many things" (v. 21). The ones who had not invested well were called "wicked" and "lazy" by the proprietor (v. 26).

God will reward the person who diligently invests his money. So, be wise with your money. Plan ahead. Save. Remember, it pays to manage your money—whether you're a big-time athlete or just a regular person in the pew.

—MOLLY RAMSEYER

POINT AFTER

Where in your finances have you been lazy? Pray today about allowing a trusted person in your life to "look" into your personal finances in order to guide you.

From the Playbook: Read Matthew 25:14–30. Which servant do you most relate to?

NFL Quarterbacks

NO. 9. JON KITNA 1997– Seattle, Cincinnati, Detroit, Dallas; 2003, NFL Comeback Player of the Year; 2006, Led NFL in completions (372); 27,293 passing yards, 152 TDs.

FAITH QUOTE: *"There's no way I would have gotten to the NFL without becoming a Christian. I was on the road to destruction."*

10. CAMP'S CHARACTER

"The fruit of the Spirit is . . . self-control."
GALATIANS 5:22–23

Walter Camp (1859–1925) took the game of rugby and morphed it into the first version of American football. By his mid-thirties, the young innovator had established many of the rules and techniques of his day. Then Camp spent nearly 50 years serving on various football rules committees that helped refine the game. He introduced—among other alterations—the scrimmage in place of a scrum, eleven players on a team, and the forward pass.

FAST FACT:
Walter Camp, known as the Father of American Football, was the head coach of the Yale football team from 1888 to 1892.

In his spare time, the busy New Haven Clock Company employee managed to write nearly 30 books, and he also penned 250 magazine articles. His topics included football (of course) and other general sports issues.

Why was Camp consumed with the whole athletics thing? He believed that young people competing in sports learn valuable lessons in self-control, leadership, and citizenship. He felt character could be forged on the football field.

Many athletes have found it to be true: Sports can teach a person some valuable, life-shaping lessons. In Galatians 5, however, we read of a better teacher of vital lessons: the Holy Spirit. He enables us to live out character qualities—like self-control—by His divine work (v. 22).

Unlike sports, where we train our bodies to master things like catching and tackling, the fruit of the Spirit works best in our lives as we yield to Him. We're filled with the Spirit and experience the fruit of the Spirit when we turn from sinful choices and choose to follow Jesus instead.

When we turn from God and pursue sin, the fruit and power of the Spirit is ineffective in our lives—and our character is less than godly.

Do you want to experience godly character? "Live by the Spirit" (Galatians 5:16). And enjoy the fruit.

—TOM FELTEN

POINT AFTER

Write down three positive character traits that you would like to possess. What is keeping you from realizing this goal? How have you been filled (influenced or controlled by the Holy Spirit through being yielded to Him), or not filled, with the Holy Spirit this week?

From the Playbook: Read Galatians 5:16–26.

TOP 100 NFL Quarterbacks

NO. 10. MATT HASSELBECK 1999– Green Bay, Seattle; 3 Pro Bowls; 26,578 passing yards, 164 TDs.

FAITH QUOTE: *"I'm playing for the Person who created me. And I'm to make Him proud and to not waste this ability He's given me."*

11. THAT'S THE SPIRIT!

"Let them praise the name of the Lord."
PSALM 148:13

For 37 years, Bob Ufer (not Bob Uecker; he's in Milwaukee) was the enthusiastic radio voice of University of Michigan football (listen to a sample at www.ufer.org). He delighted listeners with his emotional play-by-play coverage of the Wolverines. Anyone who heard him knew at once whose side he was on. He was a no-holds-barred maize-and-blue fan, and he didn't try to hide it. The loyal following that Ufer built up through the years indicates how contagious and appealing it is when a person gives himself wholeheartedly to a cause he loves.

FAST FACT:
Bob Ufer's granddaughter Heidi is married to longtime NBA player Shane Battier.

The fervor of a person like Ufer can remind us how natural it is to respond with intensity to something that is important to us—to something close to our hearts. The Scriptures give many examples of men who served the Lord with a similar kind of great enthusiasm.

For example, to mark the return of the ark of the covenant, David laid aside his royal dignity and celebrated in the streets. He "danced before the Lord with all his might" (2 Samuel 6:14). Centuries later, Jesus burned with godly zeal as He chased the money changers from the temple (Matthew 21:12). And the early church chose men like Stephen because everyone could see that the Spirit of God was working through them (Acts 6:1–5).

What about us? What do others see when they take a look at us? Do people quickly recognize by our enthusiasm that we love and serve Jesus and are filled with the Holy Spirit? Do our lives give evidence of the wholehearted praise that is called for in Psalm 148?

If Bob Ufer could get as excited about football as he did, shouldn't we get at least as excited about the fact that Someone died for our sins?

—MART DE HAAN

POINT AFTER

On a scale of one to ten with ten being high, where would you put your excitement factor in relation to your faith? How about your excitement factor for your favorite team? Which is higher?

From the Playbook: Read Psalm 148.

NFL Quarterbacks

NO. 11. STEVE BARTKOWSKI   1975–1986 Atlanta, LA Rams; 1980, Led NFL in TD passes (31); 2 Pro Bowls; 24,124 passing yards, 156 TDs.

FAITH QUOTE: *"Advancing through adversity. We see it in the apostle Paul's life. And I've seen it in my own life."*

12. FORWARD THINKING

"Joshua . . . had been Moses' aide since youth."
NUMBERS 11:28

Pat Fitzgerald described it as the "most bittersweet" moment of his life. Several days after the death of his close friend Randy Walker, Fitzgerald was given Walker's job as head coach of the Northwestern Wildcats football team.

It wasn't supposed to go this way. Walker had told Fitzgerald, one of his assistant coaches, that he was grooming him to take over several seasons down the road.

But when Walker died of a heart attack on June 29, 2006, everything changed.

Fitzgerald was pressed into head-coaching responsibilities at the young age of 31. But it's not the age of the person that matters in coaching—it's ability . . . it's character.

With that said, the people in charge of the Northwestern football team knew they were in good shape with their new, youthful coach.

He had been mentored by a successful coach who wisely chose to build into his understudy in a big way.

Moses, the leader of the Israelites, had done a similar thing while leading his people. Joshua, who had been "Moses' aide since youth" (Numbers 11:28), succeeded him as the one to guide God's chosen people.

FAST FACT:

The Northwestern Wildcats had a 7–5 record during Walker's last season as coach. Fitzgerald was 27–22 in his first four years at the helm, including two postseason bowl appearances.

As the time neared for Moses' death, he performed a final act of commissioning his understudy—he laid his hands on him. At that time a "spirit of wisdom" (Deuteronomy 34:9) filled Joshua. This supernatural gift was from God himself.

To be prepared for the tasks God is calling you to do, it is wise to seek a mentor to help you get ready spiritually. Is there a Moses in your life—someone who can come beside you to help you prepare for the future? Seek one out today. Wisdom is gained as we learn from those who walk closely with God.

—Tom Felten

POINT AFTER

If you don't already have a godly person of the same gender who is your mentor, go to God and pray for one. Ask a trusted, mature believer to suggest a good person for you to establish a mentoring relationship with.

From the Playbook: Read Deuteronomy 34:5–12.

TOP 100 NFL Quarterbacks

NO. 12. BRIAN SIPE 1974–1983 Cleveland; 1980, NFL MVP; 1979, Led NFL in TDs (28); 1 Pro Bowl; 23,713 passing yards, 154 TDs

FAITH QUOTE: *"God really started to work on me. I came to the conclusion that the Bible is the truth."*

13. THE OVERCOMERS

"God had planned something better for us so that only together with us would they be made perfect."

HEBREWS 11:40

How cold was it? It was *so cold* that seven members of the marching band were hospitalized with hypothermia. It was *so cold* that the quarterback of the losing team caught pneumonia. It was *so cold* that when the referee blew the opening whistle, it stuck to his lips.

The date was December 31, 1967—the Ice Bowl. Game-time temperature at Lambeau Field in Green Bay, Wisconsin, for the NFL championship between the Packers and the Dallas Cowboys was -13 F, with a wind chill of -48.

FAST FACT:
No fewer than 12 future Hall-of-Famers took part in the 1967 Ice Bowl.

With 16 seconds left in the game and the Pack out of timeouts, center Kenny Bowman and guard Jerry Kramer made the difference in what was perhaps the coldest pro football game ever played (in 1982, the Chargers played the Bengals in Cincinnati with a temperature of -9 and a wind chill of -59 degrees). They bulldozed a crease in the Cowboys' line so quarterback Bart Starr could wedge his way through for the winning score. Ironically, a run had been called because the offensive line had done a lousy job of protecting the frozen Starr (eight sacks). Yet those two linemen were applauded for their vital role in the final TD.

Like that Green Bay line, God's people usually struggle before coming through. In Hebrews 11, quite a few "losers" are singled out for kudos. Abraham lied twice to kings, putting his wife in jeopardy. Sarah laughed at God. Jacob was a serial schemer, thief, and liar (vv. 8–11). A closer look at the rest of the "heroes" listed in the chapter reveals even more questionable characters, including two murderers—Moses and David (vv. 23–29, 32)—and Rahab, a prostitute (v. 31).

We're no different, really. We struggle with our past, with our temptations, with our doubts. But God has great plans for us! Get back in the game! Don't let anything—from cold hearts to heated battles—stop you from overcoming for God's glory.

—Tim Gustafson

POINT AFTER

Do you let mistakes and failures stop you from trying to serve God? Why is that a mistake? (See Romans 8:31–34; Ephesians 2:8–10.)

From the Playbook: Read Hebrews 11:8–16.

TOP 100 NFL Quarterbacks

NO. 13. NEIL LOMAX   1981–1988 St. Louis, Phoenix Cardinals; 1987, Led NFL in completions (275) and yards (3,387); 2 Pro Bowls; 22,771 passing yards, 136 TDs.

FAITH QUOTE: *"Don't look any further for a role model than the Bible, where you find Jesus—the ultimate role model."*

14. ROLF'S REALIZATION

"Believe in the Lord Jesus, and you will be saved."
ACTS 16:31

A guy with a great football name, Rolf Benirschke has experienced his greatest battles off the gridiron. In 1979, in his third NFL season as a kicker with the San Diego Chargers, he developed a near-fatal condition of ulcerative colitis and nearly died. Rolf missed 12 games that year, and it took two surgeries and 80 units of blood to get him back on his feet. He was able to return to the Chargers, and he kicked for them until he retired from football in 1986.

FAST FACT:
Rolf Benirschke hosted the TV game show Wheel of Fortune *for a short time in the late 1980s. You can catch his premiere performance on YouTube.*

Twelve years later, in 1998, Rolf had a routine blood test done as part of obtaining a life insurance policy. The test revealed that he was carrying the hepatitis C virus. Doctors were nearly 100 percent sure that he got the virus from his blood transfusions!

Rolf had no idea he was sick. But since hepatitis C is deadly if it reaches its advanced stages, he embarked on a three-year program of difficult treatments that often left him feeling weak and sick.

Today, Rolf is healthy and enjoying life. But he will never forget that all-important blood test that helped save his life.

When Rolf Benirschke realized he was sick with a potentially deadly disease, it changed his life. You may be in a similar situation today. I'm talking about your *spiritual* condition.

Many people, even those who claim to be Christians, don't realize that their security is based on something false—the fact that they've done good works or are a "good person."

In Acts 16:31, we see the true basis for salvation, *"Believe* in the Lord Jesus, and you will be saved." It is *faith* in Jesus that allows us to receive salvation—nothing else. Did you realize that?

—TOM FELTEN

POINT AFTER

Write down in a few sentences why you feel you have been saved by Jesus and will spend eternity with Him. Look at the words you have written, and then read Acts 16:31 again. How does a person receive salvation? What is it based on?

From the Playbook: Read Acts 16:25–34.

TOP 100 NFL Quarterbacks

NO. 14. BOBBY HEBERT   1985–1996 New Orleans, Atlanta; 1993, Recorded longest pass completion in NFL: 98 yards; 1 Pro Bowl; 21,683 yards, 135 TDs.

FAITH QUOTE: *"You have a vacuum inside, and the Super Bowl won't fill it. Anything the world has to offer won't fill it. But Jesus will."*

15. YOU NEVER KNOW

"Why, you do not even know what will happen tomorrow."
JAMES 4:14

The life of Hall of Fame NFL player Reggie White was unexpectedly cut short when he died suddenly on the morning of December 26, 2004. He was just 43 years old.

White, known as the "Minister of Defense," was one of the greatest defenders who ever played the game of football. Throughout the 1980s and 1990s, he set multiple sack records both in college and in the NFL. After beginning his career with the old United States Football League (USFL), White moved to the NFL where he became an icon of greatness—both as a player and as a man of God. He influenced many football fans to examine the Christian faith while competing at the highest levels of his sport.

FAST FACT:
Reggie White played college football for the University of Tennessee before spending two seasons in the United States Football League and 15 years in the NFL.

Reggie's untimely death in 2004 is still a sad reminder that we never know how long our life will last. In fact, on the same day Reggie suffered a fatal heart attack, 227,898 people suddenly lost their lives when a massive tsunami slammed into several islands in Southeast Asia. Each of those people awoke the day after Christmas confident that they would live to see another day.

In the New Testament, the apostle James addressed the reality that tomorrow is uncertain. He wrote, "Now listen, you who say, 'Today or tomorrow we will go to this or that city, spend a year there, carry on business and make money.' Why, you do not even know what will happen tomorrow . . . Instead, you ought to say, 'If it is the Lord's will, we will live and do this or that'" (James 4:13–15).

No one knows for sure what tomorrow holds. There are no guarantees. But let's learn that one of the best ways to prepare for whatever the future brings is to daily surrender everything—including tomorrow—to a sovereign, loving God.

—JEFF OLSON

POINT AFTER

Do you know for sure what will happen to your soul when you die? If not, why not get ready by trusting Jesus as your Savior today.

For Further Reading: Check out the booklet *The Assurance of Salvation.* Go to www.discoveryseries.org and search for it.

 NFL Quarterbacks

NO. 15. TRENT DILFER   1994–2007 Tampa Bay, Baltimore, Seattle, Cleveland, San Francisco; 2001, Super Bowl champion; 1 Pro Bowl; 21,959 passing yards, 155 TDs.

FAITH QUOTE: *"I spend a lot of time on my knees asking God to change me. Anytime you ask God to change you, He will answer you and it's often painful."*

16. SLEEPLESS NIGHTS

"I slept but my heart was awake."
SONG OF SOLOMON 5:2

He coached college football at places like the University of Kansas, Idaho State, the University of Colorado, and Indiana University. Twenty-four years of plays swirled through his head, yet when Brian McNeely fell asleep he rarely dreamed of football—it was always about going to the mission field.

"My goal was to teach these young athletes that success on the field was temporary—the main emphasis of my teaching was about respect, justice, discipline, and other attributes of Christ, including my personal testimony of His love," McNeely recalls.

FAST FACT:
McNeely once took a head-coaching job under pressure after the former coach left the day before the season began!

While an assistant coach at Colorado in 2001, Brian felt called to take a short-term missions trip to the Thailand-Burma border. As a result, in February of 2004 he resigned from coaching and established a Christian humanitarian effort where he could serve people and also tell them about the love of Jesus Christ. Today, though he has returned to working with college athletics, his organization, Global Refuge International, is still helping people in several countries. Because of his vision, GRI provides relief and medical care for people in several countries. His burden was so transparent that two of his three grown children became a part of Global Refuge International.

What about you? What is it that keeps you up at night? Do you have a passion in your heart toward a particular thing? Consider Brian McNeely, who left a coaching position that many people would long for to follow his dream. It took faith. The book of Hebrews reminds us that faith "is being sure of what we hope for and certain of what we do not see" (Hebrews 11:1).

If today you find yourself at a crossroads, respond to God's call. It won't guarantee restful nights, but it will surely add color to your dreams!

—MOLLY RAMSEYER

POINT AFTER

Consider how Nehemiah left his position as the cupbearer of the king to go and rebuild the temple wall. Could that relate to you?

From the Playbook: Set up a plan to read the book of Nehemiah in the next month.

TOP 100 College Quarterbacks

NO. 1. DANNY WUERFFEL   College: 1993–1996 University of Florida; 1996, Won Heisman Trophy; 10,875 passing yards, 114 TDs; Pro: Drafted in the fourth round of 1997 NFL draft by New Orleans; 1997–2002 New Orleans, Green Bay, Chicago, Washington; 2,123 yards, 12 TDs; Works with Desire Street Ministries, a mission to New Orleans.

FAITH QUOTE: *"No championship or trophy can possibly compare to 'the surpassing greatness of knowing Christ Jesus my Lord' [Philippians 3:8]."*

17. NEVER COMPROMISE

Scrimmage Line:
Sticking to your commitment

*"Love the Lord your God with all your heart and
with all your soul and with all your mind."*

MATTHEW 22:37

A phrase that is used in sports by a lot of coaches from pee-wee leagues all the way to the pros is this: "Don't just go through the motions."

Coaches use this line when they feel as if their players are not 100 percent committed to the task at hand. Whether that be practicing, working out, or even sitting in a team meeting, "going through the motions" harms the team. That's why a coach will implore his or her players to be totally committed to the cause—enough so that when they play, practice, or prepare, they have their whole being involved.

FAST FACT:
Jon and Jennifer Kitna have a foundation that supports Christian causes. It is called the Jon and Jennifer Kitna Eternal Blessings Foundation.

I wonder if God is sometimes saying that we as believers in Jesus Christ are simply "going through the motions." A lot of times we do the right actions—we go to church regularly, we belong to Bible studies, we hang out with Christian people, or we might even wear a "Christian" T-shirt. Deep down, though, we know that we are just doing those things because we think we have to—not because we owe our lives to Jesus Christ.

God is looking for believers who are fully committed to Him. He wants believers who never compromise in their walk with Him—followers who are not just going through the motions.

When He finds these hearts—when he discovers believers who follow the command to "Love the Lord your God with all your heart and with all your soul and with all your mind" (Matthew 22:37), He sees men and women who are full of faith. It is this kind of faith that brings God a smile (Hebrews 11:6).

Are you ready to stop going through the motions?

—Jon Kitna

POINT AFTER

What is one thing you did this week that, now that you think back on it, was a compromise? How do you move on from that error and avoid making a similar mistake later?

From the Playbook: Read Matthew 22:34–40.

College Quarterbacks

NO. 2. HEATH SHULER 1991–1993 University of Tennessee; 1993, Finished second in Heisman Trophy race; 4,088 passing yards, 36 TDs. Drafted in first round of 1994 NFL draft by Washington; US Congressman from North Carolina.

FAITH QUOTE: *"There is nothing in life more important than the Lord and His Word."*

18. WHEN TRAGEDY STRIKES

"The Lord hears the needy."
PSALM 69:33

The winter after the 2007 National Football League season was one of the darkest periods for the Denver Broncos' franchise.

Defensive back Darrent Williams was killed in a drive-by shooting after a New Year's Eve party in Denver. Less than two months later, running back Damien Nash collapsed and died after a charity basketball game in St. Louis. The news of these two deaths rocked the Broncos' community. Mike Shanahan, the Broncos' coach at the time, said he was "speechless with sadness" after hearing the news.

Everyone knows that trials and tests of faith are more common in life than we would like them to be. But what happens when real tragedy strikes? As Christians, what's our response?

Job and David are two of the best biblical examples of faith in the midst of seemingly unbearable pain. Job was stripped of all of his wealth and most of his family, and he nearly lost his health. And while he asked many questions of God, he never lost his faith. Here is Job's response to the news that his house collapsed on his children: "The Lord gave and the Lord has taken away; may the name of the Lord be praised" (Job 1:21).

FAST FACT:
Darrent Williams accumulated 86 tackles and four interceptions in 2006. Damien Nash played in six NFL games, three for the Tennessee Titans and three for the Denver Broncos.

David, meanwhile, was a man on the run for much of his life—either from jealous King Saul or later on from his own bitter son, Absalom. The Psalms overflow with the cries of David as his life hangs in the balance. Psalm 69 is especially poignant as David struggles with life's tough challenges. Yet even then—even in the midst of life's engulfing floods (v. 1), its miry depths (v. 2) and its vain search for God, David sang of God's "sure salvation" (v. 13).

When life throws its worst at us, may our faith be this strong.

—JOSH COOLEY

POINT AFTER

Make a list of the ways God has been faithful through your trials.

From the Playbook: Set up a plan to read the book of Job in an upcoming month.

College Quarterbacks

NO. 3. DAVID CARR College: 1997–2001 Fresno State; 2001, Won the Johnny Unitas Golden Arm Award; 7,849 passing yards, 70 TDs; Pro: Drafted in first round of 2002 NFL Draft by Houston; 2002– Houston, Carolina, NY Giants, San Francisco.

FAITH QUOTE: *"Through praying, reading the Bible, or talking to my wife . . . I've tried to stay solid spiritually."*

19. REASON FOR FAITH

> " 'I know the plans I have for you,' declares the Lord,
> 'plans to prosper you and not to harm you,
> plans to give you hope and a future.' "
>
> JEREMIAH 29:11

When he was still an active NFL quarterback, current ESPN football analyst Trent Dilfer shared with *Christianity Today* readers about the vital role his Christian faith played in his life and sport ("The Glory of the Ordinary," Jeff M. Sellers, January 8, 2001).

"I couldn't be more thankful that in the past couple of years God has allowed me to deal with a great deal of change, adversity, and unknowing, because my greatest growth usually comes in times of despair," said Dilfer, whose major claim to fame in the NFL was leading the Baltimore Ravens to a win in Super Bowl XXXV.

FAST FACT:

The worst trouble came for Dilfer when he and his wife Cassandra lost their son Trevin in 2003 at the age of five after a virus infected his heart and he never recovered.

But the pathway through the NFL was not always easy for Dilfer. He was often overlooked and sometimes his skills were downplayed. Case in point: Dilfer was not re-signed by the Ravens after he led them to Super Bowl glory.

"As I've gone through great adversity professionally, God is beginning to paint a very clear picture for me of how He's drawing me closer to Him—where my heart is, what are my true deep thoughts and motives when the lights are off and nobody's around, and what that has to do with football," Dilfer added. "Are my motives to become faithful so that I'll be rewarded in football, or are my motives to be faithful so I'll just continue to trust Him?"

Can you mirror Dilfer's comments? It's not easy to do. When life hurls adversity and change at us, we are more likely to crumble rather than continue to stand tall and trust that God knows what He is doing.

When tough times come into your life, practice what Dilfer is talking about: Check your motives and keep drawing closer to God.

—ROXANNE ROBBINS

POINT AFTER

What do you have to say about how your faith affects your life? Prepare an explanation for why you have placed your hope in Jesus Christ.

From the Playbook: Read Jeremiah 29:11–14.

College Quarterbacks

NO. 4. TIM TEBOW 2006–2009 University of Florida; 2007, Won Heisman Trophy; 9,285 passing yards, 88 TDs; Drafted in the first round of the 2010 NFL Draft by Denver.

FAITH QUOTE: *"As a Christian you want to be a good influence, focus on each day, and make it the best you can."*

20. MID-COURSE CORRECTIONS

Scrimmage Line:
Being willing to make improvements

"Jonah obeyed the word of the Lord."

JONAH 3:3

The University of Miami Hurricanes football team once lost to Syracuse 66-13. After the game the coach spoke with the team, telling them, "My first year with the Dallas Cowboys we went 1-15, and 29 players on that team went on to win two Super Bowls." The next day in a team meeting the coach spoke again. He listed eight correctable mistakes on the board, indicating that the result of those mistakes was 48 points. He challenged the team to make the necessary changes. The following game the 'Canes upset No. 1 UCLA.

FAST FACT:

The year of the 66-13 loss to Syracuse, Miami went 9-3 on the season.

Correcting mistakes in life can lead us to some big successes.

Jonah ran from the Lord at great cost to himself and others. Then he made a major correction. He ran to the Lord for forgiveness and inner strength. He took the initiative to speak about his God—depending on the Holy Spirit—and left the results to God. An entire city was changed by his willingness to trust and obey God.

Another young man by the name of Evan Roberts was used by God to impact his entire country. He was a college student when the Lord impressed upon him to make some changes in his life. His pastor gathered 17 people to hear of his commitments.

1. Confess every known sin to God.
2. Make right every wrong done to others.
3. Put away every doubtful habit.
4. Obey the Holy Spirit promptly.
5. Share Christ openly.

The people in attendance that night agreed to make those commitments. They met later with others who said they too would trust the Lord to change their lives. Within six months 100,000 people had given their lives to Jesus Christ through these people.

What would happen in your area of influence if you made some mid-course corrections, using those five commitments to serve God faithfully?

—STEVE DEBARDELABEN

POINT AFTER

Think deeply and seriously about Evan Roberts' five suggested changes. Then ask God to help you implement those changes in your life.

From the Playbook: Read Jonah 3.

College Quarterbacks

NO. 5. COLT MCCOY   2006–2009 University of Texas; 2009, NCAA Quarterback of the Year, Maxwell Award; 13,253 passing yards, 112 TDs; Drafted in the third round of the 2010 NFL Draft by Cleveland.

FAITH QUOTE: *"God willing I'd like to be [successful] in the NFL, but the important thing to do is His will."*

21. "CONCUSSION" CHRISTIANITY

Scrimmage Line:
Forgiving others

*"But I tell you: Love your enemies and pray
for those who persecute you."*

MATTHEW 5:44

There has been much discussion about the problem of concussions in the NFL in recent years. One thing the NFL decided to do is to mandate that all players have "baseline" tests of brain function. That way each player will have a record of normal brain function, which can be compared with brain function in case of a concussion. This will help determine a player's readiness to return to the field after taking a hit to the head.

FAST FACT:
Helmet-to-helmet hits—a source of many concussions—can result in a player being ejected from an NFL game.

Brain function and memory loss should be a concern for those who suffer head trauma, and proper treatment should be pursued.

For Christians, is it possible that are there times when "memory loss" is a good thing? Psalm 103:12 says, "As far as the east is from the west, so far has [God] removed our transgressions from us." Does God have memory loss? No. He does choose, however, to remember our sins no more because of the redeeming work of Christ. First John 1:9 states, "If we confess our sins, [God] is faithful and just and will forgive us our sins and purify us from all unrighteousness."

Are we not to do the same when we are offended?

Remember Dory, the blue fish in the movie *Finding Nemo*? Even when Marlin, Nemo's father, tries to get rid of her several times, Dory sticks with him and helps find his son. Dory suffers from short-term memory loss, but it always seemed to be in her favor. She forgot the bad stuff.

In Matthew 5, Jesus instructs us to go the "extra mile" in loving not only our neighbors but also our enemies. When this kind of supernatural love and selective "memory loss" are demonstrated, God is glorified.

—ANDREW PROVENCE

POINT AFTER

This week think of someone you consider to be an "enemy." Seek out that person and perform a special act of kindness. If a personal encounter is not possible, pray for him or her.

From the Playbook: Read Matthew 5:38–48.

TOP 100 NFL Running Backs

NO. 1. CURTIS MARTIN 1995–2005 New England, New York Jets; 2006, NFL MVP; 2004, Led NFL in rushing (1,697 yards); 1995, Offensive Rookie of the Year; 2005, Bart Starr Award; 5 Pro Bowls; 14,101 rushing yards, 90 TDs.

FAITH QUOTE: *"Whatever gifts God has given you, you have to use them to the best of your ability. My goal in life is to please God."*

22. FAITH WITHOUT WORKS

Scrimmage Line:
Striving to live a Christlike life

"In the same way, faith by itself, if it is not accompanied by action, is dead."

JAMES 2:17

As athletes, we are under the magnifying glass each day of our careers. This is a reality and a responsibility that we face. The same expectations apply to us as Christians.

The Christian music group dc Talk introduced their song "What If I Stumble" with this line: "The greatest single cause of atheism in the world today is Christians who acknowledge Jesus with their lips, then walk out the door and deny Him by their lifestyles. This is what an unbelieving world simply finds unbelievable." This is a quotation worth thinking about.

FAST FACT:

In July 2006, Ben Utecht married Karyn Stordahl, a fellow graduate of the University of Minnesota and a former Miss Minnesota.

I love to see athletes give glory to God on the field and join in the circle of prayer at the end of the game. These acts are important and bring honor to God. The real test, though, is how we live after we leave the field of play. Does our faith have action? Do we stand firmly by the faith we so easily proclaim? Can people see our faith just by watching us interact with others?

The answers can come in many forms. How you treat your teammates and family members. How you respect those around you. Do you love unselfishly? Do you show favoritism, or are you striving to see everyone as equals? The list goes on and on. That is the beauty of this faith—it gives us so many opportunities to serve.

No matter what you are doing, if you are a Christian God has blessed you with the opportunity to shine His light. So do not keep your light under a bowl with a faith that has no works. Instead, strive to be like Christ—transformed into His likeness, so that you might walk consistently according to your beliefs, mirroring the image of Christ.

—BEN UTECHT

POINT AFTER

Are there some ways recently you were like the Christians described by dc Talk? What can you do to change that?

From the Playbook: Read James 2.

NFL Running Backs

NO. 2. LADAINIAN TOMLINSON 2001– San Diego, New York Jets; 2006, 2007, Led NFL in rushing (1,815 and 1,474); 2006, NFL Man of the Year; 2007, Bart Starr Award; 5 Pro Bowls; 12,490 rushing yards, 138 TDs.

FAITH QUOTE: *"I felt like I needed my own personal relationship with Jesus so I didn't have to rely on what my mom said all the time."*

23. GOD'S HAND

"You intended to harm me, but God intended it for good."
GENESIS 50:20

Back in 2003, when Ole Miss beat Oklahoma State in the Cotton Bowl to cap off the season with a 10-3 record, head coach David Cutcliffe was honored as the Southeastern Conference Coach of the Year. But the next year, when the Rebels struggled to finish 4-7, Cutcliffe was relieved of his coaching duties. It seemed unfair that he was fired so quickly.

A short time later, Charlie Weis, at the time the new football coach at Notre Dame, hired Cutcliffe as offensive coordinator. However, Cutcliffe had been having chest pains, and a stress test revealed the need for triple-bypass surgery. Complications following surgery brought Cutcliffe to what he called "the toughest decision I've ever had to make professionally," the decision to resign from an incredible opportunity at Notre Dame.

Unfairly fired by Ole Miss and denied by health issues the opportunity to coach at one of the premier schools in college football—how do you think he responded?

In an interview on *Sports Spectrum* Radio, Cutcliffe talked about his belief that God had these things under control. He said if he had not been let go at Mississippi, he "would have continued to ignore [the health problems]." Thinking back, he concludes, "I would have been too busy to stop, and ultimately I would have had a massive coronary. So, I do think God's hand was in it."

In the Old Testament, we read about Joseph, who experienced huge setbacks in his own life. Joseph overcame his trouble because he recognized that even in the things that were hard and unfair, God worked for good.

Are you in a difficult time in life? Like Joseph and like Coach Cutcliffe, keep trusting God. Have faith that even in this situation He can work things out for good.

—BRIAN HETTINGA

POINT AFTER

Wes Yeary of Fellowship of Christian Athletes was a friend Cutcliffe said he "leaned on hard" in response to the situation at Ole Miss. Hook up with a solid Christian friend who can help you "trust God to show you what's next."

From the Playbook: Read Genesis 50:18–21 to get Joseph's perspective on the cruel things his brothers did to him.

TOP 100 NFL Running Backs

NO. 3. SHAUN ALEXANDER   2000–2008 Seattle, Washington; 2005 NFL MVP; 2005, Led NFL in rushing and TDs (1,880 yards, 27 TDs); 3 Pro Bowls; 9,453 rushing yards, 100 TDs.

FAITH QUOTE: *"I'm always the oddball compared to everyone else. That's because I don't live by their rules. I go by God's rules."*

24. FLUTIE FAME

"Faith is being sure of what we hope for."
HEBREWS 11:1

In May 2006, the NFL's favorite Flutie decided to call it a day. Doug Flutie retired from pro football after 22 seasons of exciting quarterback scampers and passes. Although he stands just 5'10" and weighs a wispy 180 pounds, Flutie became a fan favorite because of his ability to scramble, throw on the run, and create plays.

FAST FACT:

Flutie's fabulous CFL stats include 41,355 passing yards and 270 touchdowns. He holds the pro football record of 6,619 yards passing in a single season. His drop-kick extra point in December 2005 was the first one converted in the NFL in more than 60 years.

But the man who executed a drop kick in his last NFL game decided that at age 43, it was time to hang up the cleats. Some football commentators have suggested that Flutie should be inducted into the Pro Football Hall of Fame in Canton, Ohio. That's a nice thought, but it's not likely to happen. Too many of his yards and stellar seasons occurred in the Canadian Football League—a league that has its own Hall of Fame.

To make it into the Pro Football Hall of Fame requires some serious NFL stats. The CFL just won't cut it.

In Hebrews 11, sometimes called the Hall of Faith, many Old Testament Bible characters are lifted up for something they had in common. They all *trusted* God in a way that allowed them to press on—regardless of what the future held for them.

These celebrated men and women of God lived out the idea that "faith is being sure of what we hope for and certain of what we do not see" (Hebrews 11:1). They weren't perfect. They came from different walks of life. But they were united by faith.

If you desire to know God and to follow Him, you must *trust* Him with all your heart (Proverbs 3:5–6). Without trust, your faith simply won't cut it. To get into God's Hall of Fame, faith is essential.

—TOM FELTEN

POINT AFTER

Write down five words that define a person who truly trusts God. Look them over carefully and ask yourself the following questions: How do these words reflect or not reflect my faith in God? How can I begin to trust Him more?

From the Playbook: Read Hebrews 11.

TOP 100 NFL Running Backs

NO. 4. HERSCHEL WALKER 1986–1997 Dallas, Minnesota, Philadelphia, New York Giants; 1986, 1994, Longest rushes (84 yards; 91 yards); 1987, Led NFL in yards from scrimmage (1,606); 2 Pro Bowls; 8,225 rushing yards, 61 TDs.

FAITH QUOTE: *"One thing that has helped me in my walk with Christ is seeking to avoid certain activities. All of us need to be on guard—we can all be dragged down by hanging with the wrong crowd."*

25. I AM THIRD

"Do nothing out of selfish ambition or vain conceit, but in humility consider others better than yourselves."

PHILIPPIANS 2:3

Former NFL great Gayle Sayers professed to live his life by the following creed: "The Lord is first, my friends are second, and I am third."

Sayers, who played running back for the Chicago Bears from 1965 through 1971, is most known for living out this creed in his relationship with his teammate and fellow running back Brian Piccolo. Their remarkable friendship was memorialized in the legendary movie *Brian's Song*, which was produced in 1971 and was remade in 2001.

FAST FACT:
Gayle Sayers was the NFL Rookie of the Year in 1965.

Piccolo died in 1970 at the young age of 26 after a courageous eight-month battle with a rare form of cancer—embryonal cell carcinoma. Sayers supported Piccolo till the end.

A month before cancer took Piccolo, Sayers, who had just made a courageous comeback from a potentially career-ending knee injury, expressed the following words as he accepted the NFL's Most Courageous Player Award:

"I'd like to tell you about a guy I know, a friend of mine. His name is Brian Piccolo. And he has the heart of a giant and that rare form of courage that allows him to kid himself and his opponent, cancer. He has a mental attitude that makes me proud to have a friend who spells out the word 'courage' 24 hours a day, every day of his life. Now you honor me by giving me this award. But I say to you Brian Piccolo is the man who deserves the George S. Halas Award. It is mine tonight and Brian Piccolo's tomorrow."

Sayers' speech reminds us that there is no better way to be a success than to put others before ourselves. Life is replete with situations in which we have the opportunity to put the interests of others before our own. This is the Christian way (Philippians 2:3–11). Is it your way?

—JEFF OLSON

POINT AFTER

In what situation is God inviting you to put others first? Is that easy for you or difficult? Ask God to help you with the order of things in your life.

For Further Reading: Check out Gayle Sayers' autobiography *I Am Third.*

TOP 100 College Running Backs

NO. 1. ARCHIE GRIFFIN 1972–1975 Ohio State University; Set NCAA record of 31 straight games with 100 yards or more rushing; 1974, 1975, Won the Heisman Trophy; 1973, 1974, Big Ten MVP; 1975, *Sporting News* Man of the Year; 5,589 rushing yards, 26 TDs.

FAITH QUOTE: *"I believe the ability I have is from God. It used to bother me when someone would praise me, because this is something God has given me."*

26. AWAY FROM HOME

*"Seek the peace and prosperity of the city
to which I have carried you into exile."*

JEREMIAH 29:7

When my husband, Danny, was drafted into the NFL after a stellar career at Florida in 1997, he was told, somewhat jokingly, that "NFL" stands for "Not For Long." Seems the average span of a typical NFL career is less than three years.

As it turns out, this joking statement held much more truth than originally intended. True, Danny did make it past the three-year mark, but we were never in one place for long. We moved 13 times the first four years of our marriage as he played for New Orleans, Green Bay, Chicago, and Washington. We even spent time in Europe as Danny played for the Rhein Fire in the NFL Europe league. But each city we were placed in was "Not For Long."

This is why the words of Jeremiah strike me so poignantly. He was writing to a group of Israelites who were being held captive in Babylon. Because they were away from their homes and everything familiar to them, Jeremiah instructed the Israelites to treat Babylon as if it were their home.

Jeremiah told them to build homes, have children, and pray for the peace and prosperity of the land in which they found themselves. Babylon was not home to the Israelites. In fact, they were exiled there. Why would they want to pray for

FAST FACT:

Danny and Jessica lost their home in New Orleans to Hurricane Katrina and were forced to move to Florida.

its health? Because doing so was commanded! God placed the Israelites in Babylon, just as He placed Danny and me in 13 different locations. He puts us where He wants us, and it is our job to recognize that and to pray for the peace and prosperity of our cities.

So now I count it a blessing to have had the opportunity to pray for so many different groups of people. How can you best pray for your home—or your home away from home—today?

—JESSICA WUERFFEL

POINT AFTER

Pick three specific needs of your city to pray for each day this week.

From the Playbook: Read Jeremiah 29 and 2 Kings 25.

Receivers

NO. 1. RAYMOND BERRY   1955–1967 Baltimore Colts; 1958–60, Led NFL in receptions (56, 66, 74); 1957, 1959–60, Led NFL in receiving yards (800, 959, 1,298); 1973, Inducted into HOF; 6 Pro Bowls; 9,275 yards, 68 TDs.

FAITH QUOTE: *"I believe in Jesus Christ as my all-sufficient Savior, that through faith in Him my sins are forgiven and life everlasting has been given me."*

27. WHAT COLOR IS A COACHING STAFF?

Scrimmage Line:
Practicing diversity

"May the God who gives endurance and encouragement give you a spirit of unity among yourselves as you follow Christ Jesus."

ROMANS 15:5

In the early 1970s, my family moved from Ghana, West Africa, to Michigan, where my dad became minister of a country church. It didn't seem like a big deal to us when he invited an African-American to speak at our church. Little did I know that we had moved to the heart of Klan country. Yes, *that* Klan.

I don't remember much about Harold Dungy's preaching, other than that my dad invited him back the next year. Much later, I learned that Harold Dungy had been instrumental in bringing his grandson Tony to faith in Jesus Christ. Yes, *that* Tony Dungy.

One of the absurd questions Tony Dungy heard at an early coaching interview was, "What kind of a staff are you going to put together, white or black?" What kind?! More like, "What kind of a question is that?"

Tony never forgot the question. Later, when he was hiring assistant coaches like Lovie Smith and Herman Edwards, he said that his hiring

FAST FACT:
In his rookie NFL season (1977), Tony Dungy had three interceptions on defense—and he threw two as a quarterback! In one game he threw an interception and made an interception on defense—making him the only post-merger NFL player to do that in a single contest.

decisions were about "getting good coaches and giving people a chance to come into this league."

I'm so grateful that God gives us all a chance to be a part of His family—no matter "what kind." God's Word tells us He does not want "anyone to perish, but everyone to come to repentance" (2 Peter 3:9).

It was a radical thing God did when He started building His church in the first century. Paul called it a "mystery . . . that through the gospel the Gentiles are heirs together with Israel, members together of one body, and sharers together in the promise in Christ Jesus" (Ephesians 3:6). Jews and Gentiles together? That was groundbreaking.

What color is a coaching staff? Indeed, what color is a church?

—TIM GUSTAFSON

POINT AFTER

What can you do to help make your church more diverse? How is the Holy Spirit prompting you to step out of your comfort zone?

From the Playbook: Read Romans 15:5–13.

TOP 100 Receivers

NO. 2. ART MONK   1980–1995 Washington Redskins, New York Jets, Philadelphia Eagles; 1984, Led NFL in receptions (106); 1985, Led NFL in yards per game (811.7); 3 Pro Bowls; 2008, Inducted into HOF; 12,721 yards, 68 TDs.

FAITH QUOTE: *From his Hall of Fame acceptance speech: "Coach Joe Gibbs taught me more about how to be an upstanding Christian man than anyone outside of my father."*

28. LIVING A FANTASY

Scrimmage Line:
Avoiding the dangers of sin

*"There is a way that seems right to a man,
but in the end it leads to death."*

PROVERBS 14:12

So how are you doing as a fantasy football team owner? Do you usually sweep through your league as champion? Or . . . well, let's not talk about it.

For the two of you who don't know what I'm asking about, fantasy football is a popular Internet-based game that allows average fans and even a few ex-pro football players to manage an imaginary team made up of real NFL players. Each week of the NFL season these "team owners" play against other teams in their league. Teams with the best won-loss records meet at the end of the season in a playoff to decide the eventual champion.

I have to admit that playing fantasy football is fun. I enjoy the good-natured competition and the occasional benign trash talk that takes place between team owners. It is also fun to track the performance of players you may not normally follow. That can be important if you happen to be the loyal fan of a team that has won only one playoff game in your lifetime. (Yes, the Detroit Lions.)

Fantasy football is a game within the game, sort of. There is a real component to it because it's based on the actual per-

FAST FACT:

Why do Detroit Lions fans play fantasy football? The team has one playoff victory since 1957. Between 2000 and 2009, the Lions won 42 games and lost 118 times.

formance of NFL players, but it is ultimately a fake. It's not the real deal. It has a duality about it that reminds me of sin.

Sin tends to promise to deliver something that can look so real. It offers the promise of life, but it leads to death (Proverbs 14:12). It was that way back in the Garden of Eden when the first couple ate the forbidden fruit, and it still is.

Avoid sin. What it offers doesn't work, because what it promises is nothing but a fleeting fantasy. And besides, sin is an affront to a holy God.

—JEFF OLSON

POINT AFTER

What is sin promising you today? Think about the reality behind the fantasy.

For Further Reading: Check out the booklet *The Way Back* by going to the website www.discoveryseries.org.

NO. 3. STEVE LARGENT 1976–1989 Seattle Seahawks; 1979, 1985, Led NFL in receiving yards (1,237, 1,287); 1988 NFL Man of the Year; 1988 Bart Starr Award; 7 Pro Bowls; 1995, Inducted into HOF; 13,089 yards, 100 TDs.

FAITH QUOTE: *"Our country was founded on biblical principles. Let's return to those principles: a strong work ethic, self-responsibility, personal accountability in strong families."*

29. GUILTY!

*"Sin entered the world through one man,
and death through sin, and in this way death
came to all men, because all sinned."*

ROMANS 5:12

Guilty! That's what the watching football world thought of Adam "Pacman" Jones as his face was shown on television reports throughout the summer of 2007. Jones, who was a cornerback for the Tennessee Titans at the time, was connected to a shooting crime where someone died earlier that year.

FAST FACT:

Adam Jones was the sixth player taken in the 2005 NFL Draft. Jones ended his career as a member of the Dallas Cowboys at age 25.

Reacting to the news and as the result of his investigation, NFL Commissioner Roger Goodell suspended Jones for the entire 2007 NFL season. Public perception of the former West Virginia University star made him guilty. Guilty by association—at a minimum.

It's interesting how quickly we judge athletes and public people like Adam Jones. Regardless of the crime or offense, the watching world is quick to pass judgment. That's interesting, considering that we too are guilty by association.

Our sin and guilt are not usually as public as Jones', and they may not be against the laws of our land. Yet you and I are guilty.

When the first man, Adam, chomped on the forbidden fruit in the Garden of Eden, he was guilty of sin. Unfortunately,

Adam's sin has been passed on to you and me. It's called original sin. In Romans 5:12, the apostle Paul reveals the significance of Adam's first sin—it affects all people!

Thankfully, followers of Christ don't have to live in despair, because of the significance of Jesus' sacrificial work on the cross. In verse 17 of the same chapter, Paul writes, "by the trespass of the one man, death reigned through that one man, how much more will those who receive God's abundant provision of grace and the gift of righteousness reign in life through the one man, Jesus Christ."

While we all carry the stain of our first father Adam's original sin, praise God that as followers of Jesus our stain has forever been covered by the blood of Jesus.

—ROB BENTZ

POINT AFTER

Thank God that the blood of Christ washes away the stain of original sin, and in turn, gives hope to all who trust Jesus.

From the Playbook: Read Romans 5:12–21.

TOP 100 Receivers

NO. 4. CRIS CARTER 1987–2002 Philadelphia, Minnesota, Miami; 1994, Led NFL in receptions (122); 1995, 1997, 1999 Led NFL in receiving TDs (17, 13, 13); 1994 Bart Starr Award; 1999 NFL Man of the Year; 8 Pro Bowls; 13,899 yards, 130 TDs.

FAITH QUOTE: *"My favorite verse is John 10:10, where Jesus says, 'I come that they might have life, and might have it abundantly.' "*

30. PUT DOWN THOSE CRUTCHES

*"They praised God, saying, 'We have
never seen anything like this!'"*

MARK 2:12

When Bill Parcells was the head coach of the New England Patriots, his offensive line coach's son, Rick Hoaglin, was seriously injured after slipping on a patch of ice while cross-country skiing and falling off a 100-foot cliff.

Upon his release from the hospital, Rick faced several months of painful rehabilitation to repair his left leg, which had broken in 36 places. With an electrical stimulator attached to his leg to help the broken bones fuse back together, Rick went to the Patriot's training facility daily for physical therapy. Rick's dad and the other Patriots' coaches and players cheered Rick along as he worked to regain the use of his leg.

FAST FACT:

Bill Parcells was named NFL Coach of the Year in 1986 and 1989.

The most effective therapy of all, however, resulted one afternoon when Rick encountered Coach Parcells in the hallway. "Hoaglin!" Parcells shouted, "You've been using those crutches long enough. Put those things down now and walk out of here!"

Later, Rick said he was so frightened by Parcells' command that he put the crutches down on the spot and never used them again. Although Rick knows that Bill Parcells did not heal his leg, he credits Parcells with helping him face the challenge of walking again for the first time since his accident.

In Mark 2 we learn about a paralytic man who was also aided by his friends as he sought to walk. Only in this case, they didn't scare him into walking, they brought the man to Jesus. It was not easy to do, for they had to open a hole in the roof of the house to drop the man down into where Jesus was preaching. Jesus not only healed the crippled man but what is more important, He also forgave him of his sins.

Today, thank Jesus for offering you forgiveness for your sins and helping you to walk in His love.

—ROXANNE ROBBINS

POINT AFTER

In what area(s) in your life is God asking you to "drop the crutch" and turn things over to Him in faith?

From the Playbook: Read Mark 2.

TOP 100 Receivers

NO. 4. ISAAC BRUCE   1994–2009 Los Angeles/St. Louis, San Francisco; 1996, Led NFL in receiving yards (1,338); 4 Pro Bowls; 15,208 yards, 91 TDs.

FAITH QUOTE: *"I thank God for keeping me healthy and for helping me keep my head straight and my faith in Him."*

31. ANYTHING BUT NORMAL

"Inwardly we are being renewed day by day."
2 CORINTHIANS 4:16

Super Bowl XLI on February 4, 2007, between the Indianapolis Colts and the Chicago Bears was anything but normal.

The steady rain that fell made the setting seem more like Seattle than sunny Miami. Devin Hester of Chicago returned the opening kickoff for a touchdown—which had never happened before in a Super Bowl. The first quarter alone produced four turnovers and a missed extra point. And although most experts picked the Colts to go on to win the game, no one expected how they would do it.

FAST FACT:

Peyton Manning was the MVP of Super Bowl XLI. He was 25 for 38 passing for 247 yards and one touchdown.

Peyton Manning, the big-play passing maniac with a rocket of an arm, threw only one pass for more than 20 yards. When it was all said and done, he handed the ball off more than he passed it. He even handed it off on third down. And the Colts' running backs made one big play after another against the normally tough Bears' defense.

Then there was the Colts' defense. It stuffed Chicago's running game and created the biggest play of the game—a fourth-quarter interception by Kelvin Hayden that he returned 56 yards for a touchdown. Hayden was a back-up player who made his first career pick his most memorable one.

Tony Dungy, who became the first black head coach to win it all in the NFL, summed the game up best when he said, "The Lord doesn't always take you in a straight line."

He's right. Like most important sporting events, the Christian journey is winding and unpredictable. In fact, many of the stories in the Bible tell us to expect the unexpected (see Joseph, David, and Daniel). Yet when the journey seems anything but normal, we can stay strong because we know we are ultimately moving toward a restored life with God that will take our breath away (2 Corinthians 4:16–18).

—JEFF OLSON

POINT AFTER

Where has your life taken an unexpected turn and what has it surfaced in you? How do you respond to life's surprises? Should you improve on that?

For Further Reading: Go to www.discoveryseries.org and check out the Discovery Series booklet *Why Would a Good God Allow Suffering?*

NO. 5. DERRICK MASON   1997– Tennessee, Baltimore; 2000, Led NFL in punt returns (51); 2000, Led NFL in punt return yards (662); 2001, Led NFL with longest punt return (101); 2 Pro Bowls; 11,089 yards (receiving), 59 TDs.

FAITH QUOTE: *"It's great to have Christian people around you who truly care about your outside life and your walk with God."*

32. THE COACH'S 63-YEAR LEGACY

Scrimmage Line:
Honoring marriage

"Leave your simple ways and you will live."
PROVERBS 9:6

When my wife and I learned about an affair that a friend of mine was involved in, she asked me in disbelief, "What does he want?" I knew exactly what she meant. My friend's pleasant and personable wife is—shall we say—*attractive*. What *does* he want?

That's why it was refreshing to read NFL kicker Jay Feely's blog a few years back. In it Feely—who has kicked for several NFL teams, including both New York squads—paid tribute to his grandfather, an NAIA basketball coach and devout man who passed away in early 2007. It struck me that Feely spoke little of Tom Feely's athletic record in his blog but instead honed in on his commitment to faith and family. He wrote, "Sixty-three years of faithful marriage is something to be revered."

FAST FACT:

Jay Feely began his pro career in the Arena Football League with the Florida Bobcats before signing with the Atlanta Falcons in 2001.

Revered indeed! But why is it so rare?

The ancient wise man hit on a problem we all grapple with. "Stolen water is sweet; food eaten in secret is delicious!" (Proverbs 9:17). The metaphor sounds strange in the twenty-first century, but it warns of sexual "fulfillment" outside of marriage. We crave what will not satisfy. In fact, we crave what is actually fatal. "Little do they know that the dead are there," concludes the proverb (v. 18).

Regardless of the nature of our temptation, how much better it is to exercise a bit of prudence and godly wisdom! Preparing ourselves to withstand temptation and thus avoid dangerous sins is behind wisdom's advice, "Leave your simple ways and you will live; walk in the way of understanding" (v. 6).

As Jay Feely asked, so wisely, "Do accomplishments have meaning if you sacrifice your marriage or your family to achieve them?"

I think we know the answer to that.

—TIM GUSTAFSON

POINT AFTER

The tenth commandment says, "You shall not covet" (Exodus 20:17). Why is that so difficult to follow? Why is it so important not to covet? What am I coveting today? Have I confessed it to God?

From the Playbook: Read Proverbs 9:13–18.

Receivers

NO. 7. IRVING FRYAR 1984–2000 New England, Miami, Philadelphia, Washington; 1985, Led NFL in punt return TDs (2); 1985, Led NFL in punt return yards per return (14.1); 1997 Bart Starr Award (with Brent Jones); 5 Pro Bowls.

FAITH QUOTE: *"God wants us to spend eternal life in heaven with Him. People can receive that heavenly eternal life because of what God's Son, Jesus, did."*

33. PUT THE EQUIPMENT ON

Scrimmage Line:
Preparing to battle the enemy

"Put on the full armor of God so that you can take your stand against the devil's schemes."

EPHESIANS 6:11

From our "Did You Know?" department: Did you know that in 1905 football was almost banned by the President of the United States? Eighteen players were killed and 149 were injured during that football season (at all levels of play). The reason so many died was the "flying wedge." Basically, all of the big lineman would surround the ball carrier, and they would form a V-shape and try to mow down any defender in their way. So President Theodore Roosevelt—a he-man if there ever was one—warned the colleges that were playing the game, "Either change the rules, or I'll ban the game of football."

FAST FACT:
The rules were changed on April 6, 1906, to allow the forward pass in college football. One report says the first legal forward pass in a game occurred on September 5, 1906, in a game between St. Louis University and Carroll (WI) College.

If you think about the equipment players wore in 1905, you can see another reason so many were killed or injured. Their helmet was a piece of padded leather with a chin-strap—and it was optional. No face mask, no hard plastic shell. Their shoulder pads were minimal at best. The football players of that era didn't have the equipment they needed to protect themselves against the "flying wedge."

As Christians, we face a "flying wedge" with a lot more power. But we have the equipment. It's the equipment of battle—armor for both defense and offense. It's called the "armor of God," and you can read the details about it in Ephesians 6.

It works! But too often we don't wear it. The excuses usually sound like this: "I don't have time" or "I won't need it today." Well, think about this before you head out on the field of life today: No one is going to change the rules for your safety. The opposition to our faith doesn't care about the well-being of you or your family. The enemy wants to slaughter you.

So, gear up with the equipment God gave you. Don't let the opposition use his wedge to slam you to the ground.

—Dan Deal

POINT AFTER

What excuses do *you* make for not suiting up each day with the gear God has given you? Why not decide now to suit up properly today.

From the Playbook: Check out Ephesians 6, and get the description of each piece of gear you have.

Receivers

NO. 8. BILL BROOKS 1986–1996 Indianapolis, Buffalo, Washington; 8,001 yards, 46 TDs.

FAITH QUOTE: *"My faith helps me get along with people who are not just like me."*

34. RIPPLE EFFECT

Scrimmage Line:
Guarding our relationships

"May you be richly rewarded by the Lord."
RUTH 2:12

Back in the days when football helmets were made of leather, one man changed football forever. While playing 60 minutes a game, he amassed 488 career pass receptions (200 more than his nearest competitor), 30 interceptions, and 99 touchdowns. Twice he won MVP honors, he led the NFL in receiving eight years, and he secured five straight scoring titles.

His name is Don Hutson, and he transformed football into the aerial show it is today. But he almost didn't get the chance.

FAST FACT:
In 1945, Don Hutson scored four touchdowns and kicked five extra points in a single quarter! He retired after that season.

Hutson had signed two contracts, one with the Green Bay Packers and one with the NFL Brooklyn Dodgers. The Packers had a passing game; the Dodgers did not. NFL president Joe Carr ruled that the contract with the earliest postmark—which turned out to be the Packers'—would be valid. Don Hutson was 17 minutes away from playing for a running team.

Few of us will get a chance to change a sport. But each of us can make a dramatic difference for the people in our lives. The choices we make will have an impact on those close to us in a ripple effect that can start (or prevent) a revolution for good.

In the great biblical love story, Ruth chose to stay with her widowed mother-in-law out of love for her and for God (see

Ruth 1:8–18). Her kindness to Naomi led to a series of good choices that resulted in financial salvation for both of them. But more important, God used Ruth to play a role in our spiritual salvation. She was an ancestor of Jesus!

Sports records don't matter much, but our relationships with others do! What ripple effect will your choices have on the people in your life?

—Tim Gustafson

POINT AFTER

Consider those who look up to you. Do they see that Jesus is central to your life? Do they see that you really care about them? Would others consider following Jesus based on the life you're leading?

From the Playbook: Read Ruth 1:8–18.

NO. 9. TONY HILL 1977–1986 Dallas; 3 Pro Bowls; 7,988 yards, 51 TDs.

FAITH QUOTE: *"I was looking down a dark and narrow highway, and the Lord just put His light on me. Then I could see where I was going."*

35. A NEW COLOR

*"First clean the inside of the cup and dish,
and then the outside also will be clean."*

MATTHEW 23:26

Maybe it was another failed attempt to change the team's fortunes on the field. Maybe it was a fashion statement.

For whatever reason, the 2005 Detroit Lions wore black jerseys in two of their home games instead of their traditional Honolulu blue and silver.

Perhaps the idea to sport an Oakland Raiders–style of jersey had something to do with the fact that the Lions' president at the time, Matt Millen, was a former NFL linebacker who won a couple of Super Bowls as a black-wearing Raider.

Commenting on the jersey change Millen said, "It looks great and it has a good feel." Translation—he was wishing that some of the Raider attitude would rub off when his Lions donned the black and silver.

Alas, as we all know, it didn't work.

The color of a uniform does not help a team put points on the scoreboard or make the play-offs. If a team does change its duds and then turn things around and has a winning season, it has little if anything to do with the color of its jerseys.

FAST FACT:

In their first four seasons in which they had black jerseys, the Lions were 15–49.

So, what does this have to do with you?

Just this: If you are at a place in your life where you want to turn things around, don't just focus on the externals—on the outside. Focus on what counts the most. Focus on the inside—on your heart.

Jesus once told a group of men who were obsessed with how they looked on the outside that they must *first* clean up the inside of their cups so that the outside of their cups could become clean as well (Matthew 23:25–26).

Translation—real change begins on the inside. Are you ready for a change?

—Jeff Olson

POINT AFTER

Seek out a trusted Christian friend to talk about what is going on inside of you.

For Further Reading: Check out www.discoveryseries.org to find the booklet *When Help Is Needed.*

TOP 100 Receivers

NO. 10. QADRY ISMAIL 1993–2002 Minnesota, New Orleans, Baltimore, Indianapolis; 5,137 yards, 33 TDs.

FAITH QUOTE: *"I look back on the hard times, and if the Lord wasn't with me, I wouldn't have been able to get through it."*

36. THE O-LINE

Scrimmage Line:
Pursuing faith with diligence

*"Should you then seek great things
for yourself? Seek them not."*

JEREMIAH 45:5

How many children, when they start playing football, tug on their coach's shirt and plead, "Can I be on the offensive line, coach? Please!"

None.

In the history of peewee league football, no aspiring football star ever uttered those words—ever! (I exaggerate, of course, but the number certainly cannot be very high.)

Playing the O-line is the dirtiest, toughest, and least glorious job on the football field. You never get the accolades of the quarterback or the running back. Your number only gets called when you do something wrong: "False start: Number 74! Five-yard penalty."

Seriously. Take just a moment and ponder the life of an NFL offensive lineman. A typical Sunday goes something like this: Carry as much weight as humanly possible—yet be quick-footed. Battle men your size and strength—or larger and stronger—whose sole aim is to push you around and crush your "skill" players. Do your job well, and you'll watch the quarterback or the running back get all the attention. A good offensive lineman goes unnoticed, while a poor one is known by everyone in the stadium when a touchdown is called back due to a holding penalty.

FAST FACT:
Since 1970, the average weight of an offensive lineman in the NFL has risen 62 pounds.

Offensive linemen are high-output, low-attention people.

That sounds a little like the advice the prophet Jeremiah gave to would-be-leader Baruch in Jeremiah 45:5. He encouraged Baruch to pursue anything other than personal gain. "Should you then seek great things for yourself? Seek them not." Jeremiah understood that while ambition is worthy, selfish ambition is sin.

As followers of Jesus Christ, we should have the motivation of an offensive lineman. We should work as hard as we can so we can bring honor to someone else—the Savior of all who believe, Jesus Christ.

—ROB BENTZ

POINT AFTER

Ask God in prayer to reveal the motivations of your heart. Are you pursuing excellence for yourself or for God's glory? Are you striving to earn great things for yourself or for God?

From the Playbook: Read Jeremiah 45:1–5.

TOP 100 Tight Ends

NO. 1. KEITH JACKSON 1988–1996 Philadelphia, Miami, Green Bay; 5 Pro Bowls; 5,283 yards, 49 TDs.

FAITH QUOTE: *"Once we accept Christ, we're all thrown into a position of being a role model—actually being an image of Christ."*

37. TIMES OF TRANSITION

*"Forget the former things; do not dwell on the past.
See, I am doing a new thing!"*
ISAIAH 43:18–19

Each of us will face many changes in our lives—whether it is moving to a different city or school, changing careers, or facing other types of new challenges and opportunities. In a season of transition, we often feel alone and confused.

Former NFL player Ken Ruettgers, for example, knows first-hand the conflicting emotions that arise when a professional athlete faces retirement. In his case, when football ended, Ruettgers said there were many days he would languish on the couch, depressed and uncertain what to do next with his life. After protecting the Green Bay Packers' quarterbacks as an offensive lineman from 1985 through 1996, he found it tough to know how to proceed as a 34-year-old retiree.

FAST FACT:
After graduating from USC, Ken Ruettgers was drafted in the first round by the Green Bay Packers. He was the Pack's offensive MVP in 1989.

As Ruettgers began to turn to the Lord for direction, new paths began to unfold for him. The journey differed greatly from what he had experienced in the NFL, but it took Ruettgers to a richer walk with God. Ruettgers also eventually found himself involved in a ministry more significant than he could have dreamed up for himself.

For several years, Ruettgers poured himself into the lives of other former athletes, helping them to draw closer to the Lord and to make a positive transition into the chapters that follow their sports careers. He did this through an outreach called Game's Over.

God ordains times for us to stay put and times for us to embark on something new. When it's time to move on, God says, "I am doing a new thing! . . . do you not perceive it?" (Isaiah 43:19).

In Christ, and in the power of the Holy Spirit, you are able to do things you never thought you could. You also have access to discernment through the Holy Spirit—discernment that helps you know which direction to take in times of transition.

—ROXANNE ROBBINS

POINT AFTER

Thank God for a time He did "a new thing" with your life.

From the Playbook: Read 1 Corinthians 2:9–16.

NO. 2. BRENT JONES 1987–1997 San Francisco; Appeared in 21 playoff games; 1997, Bart Starr Award (with Irving Fryar); 4 Pro Bowls; 5,195 yards, 33 TDs.

FAITH QUOTE: *"I want people to see something different about me. When I speak to a group, I don't want them to see who I am as different from what I say about Jesus."*

38. THE QB RUSH

Scrimmage Line:
Developing your spiritual life

*"Crave pure spiritual milk, so that by it you
may grow up in your salvation."*

1 PETER 2:2

The norm in the NFL used to be that a young, hotshot quarterback just coming out of college needed to sit on the bench for a few seasons before being expected to resurrect a moribund franchise.

The scenario went something like this: Use a high first-round draft choice on your franchise QB; let him stand on the sidelines, watch, and learn behind an aging veteran for two or three seasons; finally give him the reins of the team's offense; watch him lead your team out of the doldrums and into NFL prominence.

FAST FACT:
Indianapolis Colts QB Peyton Manning started all 16 games his rookie season. He threw for 26 TDs.

In recent years, that thinking has changed dramatically. NFL quarterbacks such as Matthew Stafford, Matt Ryan, Joe Flacco, and Mark Sanchez were all rushed to the field early in their professional careers.

The NFL is a win-now business. Who has time for a young leader to be groomed for future success? When a talented quarterback is drafted high, expectations are equally high for him to succeed—whether he's ready or not. NFL coaches and executives expect their young offensive leaders to grow into their role with little time for personal preparation.

As believers, our spiritual growth is not meant to be rushed like today's young signal-callers. In his first letter, the apostle Peter teaches that believers are to "crave pure spiritual milk, so that by it you may grow up in your salvation" (2:2). He is exhorting believers to pursue the pure spiritual milk of solid Bible teaching and instruction before moving on to the meat of the word. Peter knew that sound teaching and instruction is the only way to develop firmly grounded believers—preparing them biblically before moving them out into service.

Spiritual growth takes time. Seek sound teaching and training from mentors to develop your faith. Then when you are ready, you can lead the way.

—Rob Bentz

POINT AFTER

Take a few moments in prayer to tell God that you crave the "pure spiritual milk" the apostle Peter wrote about. Ask Him to give it to you through the leadership of parents, pastors, mentors, and church leaders.

From the Playbook: Read 1 Peter 2:1–3.

TOP 100

Tight Ends

NO. 3. PETE METZELAARS 1982–1997 Seattle, Buffalo, Carolina, Detroit; 1986, Led NFL in fumble returns for TD (1); 3,686 yards, 29 TDs.

FAITH QUOTE: *"I have an opportunity to have a platform to share my faith, to share Christ with people. And that's really rewarding."*

39. NO FEAR HERE

"But Moses said to God, 'Who am I, that I should go to Pharaoh and bring the Israelites out of Egypt?'"

EXODUS 3:11

J. C. Watts was born in Eufaula, Oklahoma. At 14, his athletic abilities started to get noticed. He became one of the first black players on his high school football team, but several white players quit because of it. He was called derogatory names more times than he can remember. But J. C. wasn't scared off by discrimination.

FAST FACT:

J. C. was the MVP his rookie year in the CFL's Grey Cup, the Canadian equivalent of the Super Bowl.

Watts got a football scholarship to the University of Oklahoma. As the Sooners' quarterback, he led Oklahoma to two consecutive Big Eight championships and two Orange Bowl victories. In 1981 he was drafted by the New York Jets to play running back. He said no. Why? He wanted to play quarterback, so he joined the Canadian Football League. Later, he was drafted by a new team . . . the Republican Party, for whom he served in the US Congress. For J. C. Watts, trust in God meant having no fear.

Trust in God can bring the absence of fear. Faith that God will always do the best thing can give you "no fear." Moses had some fear and trust issues when God asked him to do something that seemed kind of dangerous. But he got proof from God and said yes.

J. C. Watts has taken the life lesson of Moses to heart. Here's what he said in front of thousands at the 1996 Republican National Convention. "My faith encourages me to believe and to trust that God is still in control. 'I can't always see your hand in this, God, but I trust your heart. I trust that you're fully in control. I trust that you are going to navigate us through this.' And I've never been disappointed by God."

Proverbs 3:5 tells us to trust in God. Sound good?

—Dan Deal

POINT AFTER

What fear is blocking your path? What can you learn from J. C., Moses, and the author of Proverbs 3:5?

From the Playbook: Read about how Moses came to trust God in Exodus 3.

NO. 4. KYLE BRADY 1995–2007 New York Jets, Jacksonville, New England; 3,519 yards, 25 TDs.

FAITH QUOTE: *"Success to God is my going out and doing the absolute best I can do every day, having a good relationship with Him, and being obedient."*

40. CHANGED BY GOD

"Be transformed by the renewing of your mind."

ROMANS 12:2

Just a few days before quarterbacking the Baltimore Ravens to the NFL championship in Super Bowl XXXV in 2001, Trent Dilfer carved out a few minutes to talk to me about how God was working in his life. Here's what Dilfer said:

"I'm not afraid to say early in my career—especially in 1994 and '95—I wasn't real mature. I think many times you have to go through adversity for God to develop maturity in your life. I didn't go through many hard times in college. I went into the NFL cocky and young and thinking nothing bad was ever going to happen. It took a lot of heartache for God to get through to me and to build those characteristics into my life. It's still a work in progress but something He's definitely developing in my life.

FAST FACT:

As a junior quarterback for Fresno State in 1992, Trent Dilfer led the nation in passing efficiency.

"It comes down to trust. Who do you trust? Do you trust yourself or do you trust the One who made you? And for me, I trust the One who made me.

"I use football as an opportunity to make me a better person. The lessons I learn in football are invaluable. In my life, God has used this sport to develop character, poise, composure, calmness, peace, and trust. And those things carry over in my marriage, being a father, being a son, and then being a friend."

There's much to learn about how God changes lives when you look at how He has worked in the life of Trent Dilfer. Dilfer realized that he needed to grow up spiritually, and he allowed God to renew his mind as Romans 12 discusses.

Today, take time to figure out how God needs to work in your life. Then present your life as a living sacrifice and allow Him to renew your mind. You'll be changed for the better.

—Roxanne Robbins

POINT AFTER

List some of the ways God can use sports to help you develop "character, poise, and composure."

From the Playbook: Read Romans 12:1–8.

TOP 100 Tight Ends

NO. 5. JAY RIEMERSMA 1997–2004 Buffalo, Pittsburgh; 2,524 yards, 23 TDs.

FAITH QUOTE: *"There's nothing more important for the Christian family than the Christian father."*

41. WORDLESS WITNESS?

"Always be prepared to give an answer to everyone who asks you to give the reason for the hope that you have."

1 PETER 3:15

A lot of times when you are with your team getting ready to go out onto the field, you can tell which teammate is the most fearful by listening to who is the loudest just before the game begins. Often that loud person is the least effective when the game begins and we begin to battle our opponents.

That kind of behavior reminds me of the dog that barks incessantly while behind the fence but then tucks his tail and hides when the gate is open.

FAST FACT:

In 2003, Jon Kitna became the first quarterback in Cincinnati Bengals history to throw every one of the team's passes in a season.

We see the same to be true at times with believers. Sometimes those who talk the loudest about Jesus can't back up their talk when it's time to witness to others. Those people need to learn that what often speaks the loudest is our actions.

It's not just them. All of us need to remember that. If we would sanctify ourselves in the way we live daily, our actions would attract others to ask questions. That's when we need to be prepared to share the message of the redemption of the cross. That's when, as Peter said, we must "be prepared to give an answer to everyone who asks you to give the reason for the hope you have." But we must do this with gentleness and respect (1 Peter 3:15). Jesus said a similar thing in Matthew

5:16: "Let your light shine before men, that they may see your good deeds and praise your Father in heaven."

Both with words and with our lives, we can point people to Jesus—without being loud.

Let the light of Jesus shine in the way you live each day. People will notice, and then you'll have plenty of reason to talk of Him to others.

—JON KITNA

POINT AFTER

What is a situation where you know people will be looking at you to see if your walk lines up with your talk? If they ask you about your faith, will you be ready to explain it to them?

From the Playbook: Read Colossians 4:2–6.

TOP 100 Offensive Linemen

NO. 1. ANTHONY MUNOZ 1980–1992 Cincinnati; Started 183 games at left tackle; 1989, Bart Starr Award; 1991, NFL Man of the Year; 11 Pro Bowls; 1998, Inducted into HOF.

FAITH QUOTE: *"God has shown me that He's loving and merciful. He's got grace, but He's also a serious God."*

42. UNDERDOGS AND US

"Many who are first will be last, and many who are last will be first."

MATTHEW 19:30

The New England Patriots must have known the chilling reality of being labeled the underdog after finishing last in their division in 2000 and being picked to finish last in the 2001 season.

In the first part of the 2001 season, after a slow start of 0-3 and the injury of their starting quarterback, Drew Bledsoe, the Patriots were surely on the road to another long season. However, they were able to surprise even themselves by rallying to win 11 regular season games behind their young quarterback Tom Brady. Making the playoffs by winning the AFC East, they soon found themselves facing the heavily favored St. Louis Rams in Super Bowl XXXVI on February 3, 2002. With a successful last-second field goal, the Patriots won it all and thus became labeled a "worst to first" team.

FAST FACT:

Patriots quarterback Tom Brady, who won his first nine playoff game starts, was a sixth-round pick in the 2000 draft. He was the 199th player taken in the draft that year.

Have you ever felt like "the predicted loser"? If so, you are not alone. If anyone knew about coming from behind or being overlooked or being the unlikely hero, it was Jesus and His disciples. Jesus himself was underrated because he was from Nazareth (John 1:45–46) and because He was the son of a carpenter (Matthew 13:55).

And Jesus always seemed to recruit His team from those left standing in line in gym class after everyone else was chosen.

He picked stench-ridden fishermen and greedy tax collectors. They didn't appear to be leaders or standouts or to even have much talent, but they did have one shared characteristic—a willingness to obey their Teacher!

Whenever you feel disregarded or marginalized, or the odds don't seem to be in your favor, remember that no matter what the world says about you, you are on the greatest team of all time. Take heart—the God of the universe picks the underdog. And in the end, He wins!

—MOLLY RAMSEYER

POINT AFTER

Thank God today for the strength that is available to you when you ask in prayer. Thank Him for your "lot" in life and rejoice in His acceptance.

From the Playbook: Read about underdog David in 1 Samuel 16:6–7, 11–13.

TOP 100 Offensive Linemen

NO. 2. DWIGHT STEPHENSON 1980–1987 Miami; 1985, NFL Man of the Year; 5 Pro Bowls; 1998, Inducted into HOF.

FAITH QUOTE: *"As a lonely young man in college, I gave my life to Jesus—and He gave me my life purpose."*

43. ALL OF YOUR HEART

"God, whom I serve with my whole heart in preaching the gospel of his Son, is my witness."

ROMANS 1:9

It's not just the *talent* of an athlete that makes the difference. A 2006 AFC Divisional playoff game between the Pittsburgh Steelers and the Indianapolis Colts is a powerful example of the fact that it is the *heart* of the athlete that counts the most.

Going into the game, the Colts were loaded with talent. They were the No. 1 seed in the AFC, coasting into the playoffs after winning their first 13 games of the season. Peyton Manning, guiding his star-studded offense, was having another MVP caliber year, and the Colts finally had a vastly improved defense.

FAST FACT:

The Steelers are the only NFL team to put their logo on only one side of the helmet. That tradition began in 1962.

On the other side of the ball, the Steelers had just squeaked into the playoffs as the last Wild Card team. Even though the Steelers had won their first playoff game 31-17 over Cincinnati, the Colts had already shown they were the more talented team by beating Pittsburgh soundly earlier in the season 26-7.

But this game was a different story.

What the underdog and visiting Steelers lacked in talent they more than made up for with their heart. The Steelers jumped out to a 21-3 lead and held off a late fourth-quarter rally to beat the Colts 21-18. That paved the way for their eventual 21-10 win over the Seattle Seahawks in Super Bowl XL in Detroit.

The Steelers' performance is a powerful picture of how to serve God. No matter how little or much "talent" we think we have been blessed with, God wants us to serve Him whole-heartedly. After all, He's the one who gave us the right amount of ability to do what He wants us to do. We are to live for Him with everything we've got—serving Him with our "whole heart" (Romans 1:9). Remember, Jesus said to love God with *all* of our heart (Luke 10:27).

—JEFF OLSON

POINT AFTER

In what area of your life are you living half-heartedly? What can help you to turn that other half around?

For Further Thinking: Check out the film *Facing the Giants* (Destination Films, 2006).

TOP 100 Offensive Linemen

NO. 3. JACKIE SLATER   1976–1995 Los Angeles/St. Louis Rams; 1996, Bart Starr Award; 7 Pro Bowls; 2001, Inducted into HOF.

FAITH QUOTE: *"I asked Jesus Christ to come into my heart and forgive me of my sins and make me the man He wanted me to be."*

44. DRESSIN' UP

*"Clothe yourselves with compassion, kindness,
humility, gentleness and patience."*

COLOSSIANS 3:12

Legendary Dallas Cowboys coach Tom Landry always wore a suit, tie, and his trademark fedora as he paced the sidelines. Things have changed in the NFL since Landry led the Cowboys in the '70s and '80s. Today, the NFL office requires coaches to wear logo-emblazoned sportswear.

During the 2006 NFL season, though, a pair of NFL coaches hauled out their finest duds. Mike Nolan of the San Francisco 49ers and Jack Del Rio of the Jacksonville Jaguars each donned a sport coat and tie on the sidelines of their NFL games. They could not, however, make it a habit. The NFL rules don't allow it; the league likes its coaches to model NFL-sponsored hats and shirts that bear the logo of a company with which it has a contract. The league gave Nolan and Del Rio limited opportunities to dress up. Nolan wore his coat and tie to honor the regular attire of his father, former NFL coach Dick Nolan. Del Rio told the press he spruced up because it had a "neat, professional look."

FAST FACT:
Mike Nolan's father, Dick Nolan, coached the San Francisco 49ers from 1968–75 and the New Orleans Saints from 1978–80— in a suit and tie.

As followers of Jesus, Christians should also be concerned about their "look." But I'm not talking about a suit and tie. Not even a pair of khakis and a button-down or polo. Believers can find their "approved" clothing list on the pages of the Bible.

The apostle Paul wrote to the church in Colosse with instructions on the appropriate dress code for believers. In Colossians 3:12, Paul explains it: "Clothe yourselves with compassion, kindness, humility, gentleness and patience."

As followers of Christ, we have a responsibility to be clothed with attributes that serve and minister to people both inside and outside the church. We are to be covered in compassion. And our lives must be clothed in kindness, humility, and gentleness.

Are you dressed up?

—Rob Bentz

POINT AFTER

Through prayer, ask God to clothe you with compassion, kindness, humility, gentleness, and patience. At the end of the week, take a few moments to journal how God answered your prayer.

From the Playbook: Read Colossians 3.

TOP 100 Offensive Linemen

NO. 4. BRUCE MATTHEWS 1983–2001 Houston/Tennessee; NFL Record 292 starts (1983–2001); 14 Pro Bowls; 2007, Inducted into HOF.

FAITH QUOTE: *"I thank the Lord Jesus Christ for blessing me, and I fully recognize Him and what God has done for my life."*

45. TRUE GREATNESS

"Whoever humbles himself like this child is the greatest in the kingdom of heaven."

MATTHEW 18:4

The eyes of the world seem to be forever scanning the horizon, looking for the next great athlete to surface and shock us all. Recruiters, journalists, publicists, and sports agents are always in pursuit of those who are bigger, faster, stronger, and greater than any athlete we have yet seen. And when they find these rare diamonds, the talk shows begin to buzz with the question, "Who will be the greatest?"

FAST FACT:

Between 2000 and 2010, the No. 1 NFL draft picks: Courtney Brown, Michael Vick, David Carr, Carson Palmer, Eli Manning, Alex Smith, Mario Williams, DeMarcus Russell, Jake Long, Matthew Stafford, and Sam Bradford.

NFL Insider once featured an article asking who would be the Top 10 young superstars in the NFL in the next ten years. Contributing editor and former personnel guru of the Dallas Cowboys, Gil Brant, was ready with his response. He listed athletes that possess the rare skills needed to become great: speed, strength, talent, and size.

This question of greatness is not a new one. A similar issue was raised nearly 2,000 years ago. The Bible records the story of Jesus' disciples asking Him the question "Who of us will become the greatest?" Jesus answered quite differently from any talk-show host. He told the disciples not to seek greatness at all, but rather to become humble, as a child (Matthew 18:1–4).

Success to God is not based on your fame, or even your skill, but rather on your love for Him and others.

Do your motives stem from a desire to be recognized? Do you find yourself looking for greatness in your personal achievements, or do you seek God's approval through humbly serving others? The eyes of the Lord are not searching for the next great athlete, but rather, "the eyes of the Lord range throughout the earth to strengthen those whose hearts are fully committed to him" (2 Chronicles 16:9).

Are you "next" in that category?

—MOLLY RAMSEYER

POINT AFTER

Write down times throughout the day when you feel overlooked by the world as well as the opportunities you have to serve others.

From the Playbook: Read Matthew 20:20–28.

TOP 100 Offensive Linemen

NO. 5. STEVE WISNIEWSKI 1989–2001 LA/Oakland Raiders; 8 Pro Bowls.

FAITH QUOTE: *"Since the day I trusted Jesus, I've been a new creation in Christ. I've had a hunger to be in God's Word and a hunger to tell others about Jesus.*

46. FINISH THE RACE

Scrimmage Line:
Striving to reach the goal

*"I press on toward the goal to win the prize for which God
has called me heavenward in Christ Jesus."*

PHILIPPIANS 3:14

I believe what separates the great athletes—Kobe Bryant, Peyton Manning, Roger Federer, and the like—from everybody else is one simple thing: The ability to finish strong. No matter the score, be it a great deficit, a great lead, or a tight race, the great athletes save their best for when it means the most.

FAST FACT:

In college, Jon Kitna was a first-team All-American at Central Washington University, which at the time was an NAIA school. It is now NCAA Division II.

Notice, for instance, that when the game is on the line, more likely than not the Los Angeles Lakers have the ball in Kobe's hands for the last shot. We all know how often Peyton has led his team downfield in the game's closing moments. And who in his right mind would want to face Federer in a tiebreak with the US Open on the line?

This is the kind of toughness we need in our mind-sets as Christians: An ability to forget the past—whether it was a great time of trouble or a time of exaltation—and then press on toward what God has for us right now. Paul put it like this: "Forgetting what is behind and straining toward what is ahead, I press on toward the goal to win the prize for which God has called me heavenward in Christ Jesus" (Philippians 3:13–14).

Too many times we get to a point where we feel as if God could never forgive us—that our errors of the past continue to stop our progress. But if we do feel that way, we must remember that this is why Christ died and why we now have repentance. No matter what the circumstance, God can forgive!

So my encouragement for you is to let the past be the past. As one of my former coaches, Marvin Lewis, often said, "Don't let the last decision, good or bad, affect your next great decision."

To win the race we have to look ahead—and finish the race!

—JON KITNA

POINT AFTER

What circumstance is making you think you can't finish well? Would it help to think of Jesus and what He endured during the final days before His crucifixion?

From the Playbook: Memorize Philippians 3:13–14.

Offensive Linemen

NO. 6. KEVIN MAWAE 1994–2009 Seattle, New York Jets, Tennessee; 8 Pro Bowls; Served as president of the NFL Players Association.

FAITH QUOTE: *"I have experienced joy in sorrowful circumstances, and I am strengthened by God's Word each day."*

47. LET YOUR FAITH HANG OUT

"I am not ashamed of the gospel, because it is the power of God for the salvation of everyone who believes."

ROMANS 1:16

Although many fans wondered if—during his years with the lowly Detroit Lions—quarterback Jon Kitna might have been ashamed of the team he played for, Kitna is definitely not a man who is ashamed of his faith. He is a follower of Christ, something he does not hide from anyone.

FAST FACT:

In 2004 John Kitna was fined by the NFL for wearing a cross on his hat in a postgame interview. In the next couple of weeks, a Cincinnati store sold several thousand caps just like the one Kitna wore.

Kitna will be the first to tell anyone who will listen that it was his relationship with Jesus Christ that got him through the trials of his life and directed him on his path to the NFL.

Outspoken Christian athletes run the risk of being misunderstood, so they take a risk in talking about their faith in the public market. For instance, some skeptics think being a person of faith is a sign of weakness, and thus they label believers in Christ as nonaggressive. But Cory Schlesinger, one of Kitna's teammates when they both played for Detroit, and who happened to be one the toughest fullbacks to ever play in the NFL, said, "I don't think that guy is soft at all." Schlesinger continued, "There are definitely a lot of men of faith who are labeled as soft, but that is not the case. They are playing for something other than themselves."

It's true. Win or lose, Christian athletes are competitive and dedicated in their mission because they are playing for something bigger. While most athletes play for money or fame or just for the love of the game, followers of Christ are ultimately playing to glorify God (1 Corinthians 10:31). That is what sets them apart.

Are you a believer? Don't be wimpy or shy about your faith. And whatever you do for a living, give it everything you've got. That alone can bring attention and glory to your God in ways you may not realize.

—JEFF OLSON

POINT AFTER

What is one thing you could do to share your faith where you work?

For Further Reading: Check out the booklet *How Can I Break the Silence?* at www.discoveryseries.org.

TOP 100 Offensive Linemen

NO. 7. TONY BOSELLI   1995–2001 Jacksonville Jaguars; 5 Pro Bowls

FAITH QUOTE: *"I thank God that He's given me the opportunity to touch kids through Him and to speak a message of hope to them."*

48. WINDS OF CHANGE

"We will no longer be infants, tossed back and forth by the waves, and blown here and there by every wind of teaching."
EPHESIANS 4:14

Many years ago, a football coach by the name of Bill Walsh introduced the West Coast Offense into the NFL. The faithful implementation of this new and exciting offense brought Walsh and the San Francisco 49ers great success in the 1980s. The Niners' offensive scheme truly revolutionized the NFL. Team after team and coach after coach followed in Walsh's footsteps, seeking to establish the West Coast Offense with their team. The West Coast Offense was all the rage!

Fast-forward a few decades to today. Just a few NFL teams still run some form of the West Coast Offense. A "vertical passing game" is more in vogue in today's National Football League. And the Wildcat offensive set has grown in popularity. And who knows if new innovations such as the A-11 will ever appear in the NFL?

Trends change—often dramatically!

In Ephesians 4:14, the apostle Paul exhorted the believers in Ephesus not to be blown here and there by the winds of culture. He encouraged them to stand strong in the Truth—and thus be unified as a community of faith.

FAST FACT:
Bill Walsh coached the 49ers to three Super Bowl titles with his new offensive philosophy. It is believed that Bill Parcells first labeled Walsh's plays the West Coast Offense.

Too often you and I face the temptation to follow the winds of change that blow through our culture. Sometimes we feel pulled to follow a particular Bible teacher who, while intriguing and interesting, is not biblical. Or we may be encouraged to submit to a particular theological point of view that is contrary to traditional Christian doctrine. And at times we are even challenged to take part in a specific activity that we know is contrary to the Word of God. Trends blow through the church, and we need to have the strength to resist them if they violate orthodox biblical truth.

Be faithful to what you know to be true. Keep reading and studying the Scriptures. Keep praying and memorizing God's Word—that will help you stand firm against the strong winds of our culture.

—ROB BENTZ

POINT AFTER

Ask God through prayer to protect your heart and mind from being swept up in the waves and the winds of our culture that are contrary to the truth of the Bible. Pray specifically for strength and discernment.

From the Playbook: Read Ephesians 4:1–15.

TOP 100 Offensive Linemen

NO. 8. GUY MCINTYRE 1984–1996 San Francisco, Green Bay, Philadelphia; 5 Pro Bowls.

FAITH QUOTE: *"People will listen to you because you're a football player. You have to believe that God's Word won't fall on deaf ears and that you're planting a seed."*

49. THE GREEN-EYED MONSTER

"Who can stand before jealousy?"
PROVERBS 27:4

It started in 1981 before George Halas hired Mike Ditka to coach the Chicago Bears. Buddy Ryan was the defensive coordinator at the time, and many of the Bears had signed a letter asking Halas to sign Ryan instead as the new head coach.

The tight bond between Ryan and his defenders is indicated by this story, which occurred after Ditka was named head coach: Once, while in a meeting with members of the defense, Ditka made a comment about them. Ryan snapped to Ditka, "Get away from my team. These are my players."

Four years later, the Bears went on to win Super Bowl XX. Meanwhile, Ryan announced before the big game that he was going to become the head coach of the Philadelphia Eagles. In the next few seasons, the Eagles and Bears played four times, and each game was billed as a grudge match between Ryan and Ditka. While Ditka didn't say much, Ryan talked all kinds of trash against Ditka and the Bears. Green wasn't just the Eagles colors, it appears.

After saying nothing for four years, Ditka spoke out after the infamous Fog Bowl at Soldier Field on New Year's Eve 1988. A thick fog rolled in off Lake Michigan for this game, which the Bears won 20-12. Said Ditka in postgame com-

FAST FACT:
Mike Ditka is an NFL Hall of Famer who also played baseball and basketball at the University of Pittsburgh from 1958 through 1960.

ments, "I'm a duck, and I let his words roll off my back like water off a duck's back. He's just jealous."

Proverbs 27:4 asks, "Who can stand [against the force of] jealousy?" It is a powerful force, and it fueled one coach's revenge against his former team.

Jealousy can fuel a lot of other things in our lives too. Bad things. Paul lists it as one of the "acts of the sinful nature" (Galatians 5:19), so we know it is destructive to a relationship. Don't let that emotional, green-eyed monster rule your life. You will fall.

—DAN DEAL

POINT AFTER

Who do you look at with green eyes—wishing you had what they have? How can the Ditka-Ryan feud help you to see the fruitlessness of jealousy?

From the Playbook: Read Psalm 27, Ecclesiastes 9, or 1 Corinthians 3.

Offensive Linemen

NO. 9. JEFF SATURDAY 1999– Indianapolis; 4 Pro Bowls.

FAITH QUOTE: "When Christians serve people in need, you can really see Christ alive."

50. GIVE HIM TIME

*"Don't let anyone look down on you because
you are young, but set an example."*

1 TIMOTHY 4:12

Green Bay Packers linebacker Brady Poppinga didn't have a very good start to the 2006 NFL season. After three games, Poppinga had dropped potential interceptions. He had missed tackles he should have made. He had been burned on a 57-yard reception. The second-year linebacker was not playing anywhere near the potential the Green Bay Packers saw in him.

FAST FACT:

The Packers liked Brady Poppinga enough to sign him to a deal that was scheduled to pay him $17 million through 2012.

But the Packers didn't bench him. They stuck with their young defensive prospect.

Behind Poppinga on the Packers' depth chart was Ben Taylor, a very capable NFL veteran of five years. The easy thing would have been for first-year head coach Mike McCarthy to go with the results of the veteran instead of building for the team's future with Poppinga's potential. McCarthy and his staff didn't waver. Poppinga remained the starter. Why? Because the Packers brass believed the only thing he needed was experience. They were right, for Poppinga recorded 107 tackles over the following three seasons for the Packers.

The apostle Paul must have had similar feelings about his young understudy, Timothy. In 1 Timothy 4:12, Paul writes, "Don't let anyone look down on you because you are young, but set an example for the believers in speech, in life, in love, in faith and in purity."

Regardless of Timothy's age, Paul knew that his understudy was a man of God. He knew that Timothy was ready to set a godly example to the people of Ephesus. He recognized Timothy's potential.

Young men and women may not have the life experience many assume is needed in a spiritual leader, but if their lives are marked by love, faith, and purity, then give them time. Then watch them "set an example" as Paul expected Timothy to do.

—ROB BENTZ

POINT AFTER

Take a moment to examine your life. Does your speech, life, love, faith, and purity set an example for others? Ask God through prayer to forgive you for the sin in your life in these areas, and to clean up the rough spots for His glory.

From the Playbook: Read and memorize 1 Timothy 4:12.

TOP 100 Offensive Linemen

NO. 10. TARIK GLENN   1997–2006 Indianapolis; 3 Pro Bowls.

FAITH QUOTE: *"Before I became a Christian, criticism really got to me. This all changed when Christ entered my life, and I began following and obeying the Word of God."*

51. FINAL PLAY

*"Man is destined to die once, and after
that to face judgment."*
HEBREWS 9:27

The score was 20-19 as the teams lined up for the final play. The snap was crisp, the placement true. A powerful foot swept through the ball, lofting it goalward. And then, Al Michael's memorable call: "No good! Wide right!" A narrowly missed field goal made the New York Giants Super Bowl XXV champions in 1991.

It was 47 yards, certainly no chip shot. And the Buffalo Bills had squandered numerous opportunities to seize the game. But it's a kick that professional kickers will tell you they should make.

The play came to define Scott Norwood's career, but he refused to let it define *him*. Through hard work and help from those who loved him and knew him best, he has become a successful family man—something vastly more important that converting a kick.

FAST FACT:
Scott Norwood, a Division I-AA kicker (James Madison University), scored 670 points in the NFL.

How many of us could stand up to the sort of standard imposed on Scott Norwood? Yet there's one crucial standard all of us will be measured against. And we'll all fail to meet it!

"Man is destined to die once," says the Bible, "and after that to face judgment" (Hebrews 9:27). God's Word also tells us, "There is no one righteous, not even one" (Romans 3:10). In effect, we are all spiritually "No good!" We're all "Wide right!"

Mercifully, that's not the end of the story. "Christ was sacrificed once to take away the sins of many people," says Hebrews 9:28. And "Everyone who calls on the name of the Lord will be saved" (Romans 10:13).

Mercifully for the Buffalo Bills, Super Bowl XXV will some day be forgotten. The more important question is this: Will your sins be forgiven and forgotten? Or will you be regretting them for eternity?

It's that serious! And it's your call.

—TIM GUSTAFSON

POINT AFTER

How do you define failure? How do you think God defines it? Is there a difference? Have you ever acknowledged your sins to God and asked for His forgiveness?

From the Playbook: Read Hebrews 9.

TOP 100 Kickers

NO. 1. GARY ANDERSON   1982–2004 Pittsburgh, San Francisco, Minnesota, Tennessee; 1985, Led NFL in field goals made (33); 1998, Led NFL with 35 of 35 field goals and 59 of 59 extra points; 1998, Led NFL in points (164) and extra points made (59); 4 Pro Bowls; Points, 2,434; Field goals, 538; Extra points, 820.

FAITH QUOTE: *"It's important to let kids know about our bad times so they can see how God can make a difference."*

52. TRUE VICTORY

*"Whatever you do, work at it with all your heart,
as working for the Lord, not for men."*

COLOSSIANS 3:23

As we know, in sports there will always be a winner and a loser. The whole idea of sport is to determine who is the better team or individual. It is a great concept, because it's so nice and clean in regard to competition. Whether you are a team of 80 people, such as a football team; or if you are a team of one, like a golfer, at the end of each contest you have feedback as to where you stand in comparison to others.

FAST FACT:

Jon Kitna broke into the NFL with Seattle in 1997 and played for four teams: Seattle, Cincinnati, Detroit, and Dallas.

The problem we can all face with competition comes when we wrap our identity in these results. You see, while the world is concerned only with who won and who lost—the end result—God is concerned with *how* you won or lost. The world judges us in comparison to others, but God sees us each individually and uniquely.

Jesus asked His disciples who the people said He was, and they gave answers. Then He asked—and this is more important—who they said He was (Matthew 16:13–20). God is concerned and judges us on what is not seen—our heart, mind, and attitude. When Peter said, "You are the Christ, the Son of the living God" (v. 16), Jesus praised him and called him "blessed." Peter was honored for standing out and standing up for what was correct.

We can win on the scoreboard of life, but maybe we cut corners or didn't give our best. In relation to Colossians 3:23, we lost. Conversely, we can lose on the scoreboard of life after giving it all we had and living with integrity. In that case, we can be sure that God would say to us, "Well done, good and faithful servant" (Matthew 25:21).

So, no matter what our earthly circumstances are—whether it is a 2-14 season or a season that takes us to the playoffs—we can be winners in God's eyes, and His is still the only opinion that truly matters.

—Jon Kitna

POINT AFTER

Think back over the work you did today. Did you do everything heartily, as to the Lord? What was one thing you feel you could improve on?

From the Playbook: Read Matthew 16:13–20.

TOP 100 Kickers

NO. 2. JOHN CARNEY 1988– Tampa, San Diego, Rams, New Orleans, Jacksonville, Kansas City, NY Giants; 1994, Led NFL in points (135); 1994, Led NFL in field goals made (34); 2 Pro Bowls; Points, 2,044; Field goals, 473; Extra points, 635.

FAITH QUOTE: *"When I think of two words that describe my life and career, they are* faith *and* perseverance. *Faith that God has a plan for my life. We must have the courage to fail and the perseverance to succeed."*

53. BE DILIGENT

Scrimmage Line:
Sticking to godliness

"The plans of the diligent lead to profit."
PROVERBS 21:5

They're not the fastest, the strongest, or the biggest players on the gridiron, but NFL fullbacks may have the toughest job on the field. They're expected to take punishing hits, block defensive ends twice their size, run precise routes for the short pass, protect the quarterback, and take the handoff up the middle while behemoths threaten to bury them under a mound of humanity. An NFL fullback is an all-around amazing athlete!

FAST FACT:
For nine consecutive seasons, Lorenzo Neal paved the way for a 1,000-yard rusher.

Lorenzo Neal, who enjoyed a 16-year NFL career as a fullback with New Orleans, the New York Jets, Tampa Bay, Tennessee, Cincinnati, San Diego, Baltimore, and Oakland is one of those amazing athletes. Neal once told me that the key to his success during the brutal football season was his diligence during the offseason. That's when he would push himself through grueling boxing sessions to prepare for what was to come during the season, gradually improving his upper body strength, agility, and endurance. That's why he could play effectively in the NFL until he was 38 years old. His diligence prolonged his career to more than five times the length the average athlete spends in the pros.

Similarly, in our walk with Christ, diligence is a key component in keeping spiritually fit. Consistently studying the Bible and putting its principles to use will condition us to face whatever may come our way, whether it's an unexpected obstacle in our path or a temptation that threatens to overwhelm us. Spending time praying, getting help from other believers, and worshiping regularly are activities that keep us on track.

Staying diligent will make a difference in the long run as we seek to stay in shape spiritually.

—JENNA SAMPSON

POINT AFTER

What can you do every day to start being more diligent in your walk with Christ?

From the Playbook: Read about a young man who wasn't willing to let big things get in his way, and he later became king. Start at 1 Samuel 17.

NO. 3. MATT STOVER 1991–2009 Cleveland/Baltimore, Indianapolis; 1994, 2006, Led NFL in field-goal percentage (92.9, 93.3); 2000, Led NFL in field goals made (35); 1 Pro Bowl; Points, 2,004; Field goals, 471; Extra points, 591.

FAITH QUOTE: *"I have found that Jesus alone can fill the void we all have in our lives."*

54. DESERT HOPE

"Since we have such a hope, we are very bold."
2 CORINTHIANS 3:12

Back in 2006, before the Arizona Cardinals were good—before they had reached the heady heights of the Super Bowl, the team announced the signing of free-agent running back Edgerrin James to a four-year contract. When that happened, the desert was abuzz!

With the Edge in the backfield, former NFL Most Valuable Player Kurt Warner under center, and a stable of fleet young receivers lining up to haul down passes, it finally appeared that the long-suffering Cardinals had legitimate hope of making some postseason noise.

On the day of the signing, Cards fans were so excited they crashed the team's website with the sheer volume of visitors!

Cardinals' season tickets also became a hot commodity. Team official Ron Minegar told the *Arizona Republic*, "I don't think they'll [ticket staff] be able to process everything that's come in today." Suddenly, there was hope in the desert!

FAST FACT: *The Arizona Cardinals not only got better but they also made it to the Super Bowl in 2009 behind Kurt Warner.*

We all need hope that goes far deeper than whether our NFL team will be any good. In 2 Corinthians 3, the apostle Paul wrote about the hope he had. In his letter to the church in Corinth, he told of the glorious nature of the ministry he shared with them—spreading the gospel.

Paul spoke of the new covenant—a new relationship between God and man made possible only through the death and resurrection of Jesus. This covenant of grace is the one that gives hope to all who believe in Jesus.

This covenant is a reality for believers today, just as it was in the time of the New Testament. The gracious relationship between God and man gives believers true and certain hope—hope of everlasting life. And that gives Paul—and you and me—boldness to take the good news of new life in Jesus to the world.

—ROB BENTZ

POINT AFTER

Read the From the Playbook selection below, and highlight at least two things from this passage that give you great hope!

From the Playbook: Read 2 Corinthians 3:7–18.

TOP 100 Kickers

NO. 4. JASON ELAM   1993–2009 Denver, Atlanta; 2000, Led NFL in extra points (49); 2001, Led NFL in field goals made (31); 3 Pro Bowls; Points, 1,983; Field goals, 540; Extra points, 436; Author, missionary pilot.

FAITH QUOTE: *"One of the aspects of our faith that we're definitely called by God to do is encourage our brothers and sisters. One way I encourage others is by missionary work in Alaska."*

55. LIVING LARGE

"I have called you friends."
JOHN 15:15

In the 2004 film *Friday Night Lights*, head coach Gary Gaines of Permian High School in Odessa, Texas, gathered his team together in the locker room shortly before the biggest game of their lives. Looking them straight in the eye, he said to the players, "Gentlemen, the hopes and dreams of an entire town are riding on your shoulders. You might never matter more than you do right now. It's time."

FAST FACT:

Between 1965 and 1991, Permian High School won six Texas state high school football championships.

Wow! What a speech! If I were one of those players, I would have felt as if I was about to become a part of something really big.

I know. I know. It was only a movie. But as I listened to those words, I felt that it pointed out a deep desire within every one of us. Deep down inside we all want to know that we are a part of something large—something larger and more important than we are.

As Christians, we are part of such a thing! We all have an important role to play in God's larger story of redemption and restoration. Jesus said that He didn't consider those who follow Him as His servants, because servants aren't involved in their master's business. Instead, he regarded those who followed Him as His "friends" (John 15:15).

It's late in the story, yet God has a unique role for every one of His "friends" to step into. Accepting God's invitation to take our place in the business of saving and restoring people who are lost and who need redemption in Jesus Christ is the largest thing we will ever do or be a part of.

It's time to live large. Do you know what your role is?

—JEFF OLSON

POINT AFTER

How are you looking to find your role?

For Further Study: Check out www.epicreality.com for an insightful look at God's larger story and how you can become a part of it.

Kickers

NO. 5. JASON HANSON   1992– Detroit; 1995, Led NFL in extra points (48); 2 Pro Bowls; Points, 1,835; Field goals, 427; Extra points, 554.

FAITH QUOTE: *"Many times you end up where God wants you to be by persevering, being faithful."*

56. THE LEGACY OF GERALD FORD

Scrimmage Line:
Establishing spiritual traditions

"Trust in the Lord with all your heart."
PROVERBS 3:5

With the death of President Gerald Ford at age 93 in December 2006 came the opportunity for Americans to be reminded of the man who steadfastly led the United States out of a very difficult time following the resignation of President Richard Nixon in August 1974. Eloquent eulogies given at President Ford's state funeral told of his work ethic, his integrity, his honesty and openness, and of his devotion to his wife Betty and to the Lord.

FAST FACT:
Gerald Ford played center and linebacker for the University of Michigan—national champs in 1932 and 1933.

Many people knew that Mr. Ford spent a majority of his life in public service before becoming president. But few knew that sports and his Christian faith had also played an integral part in shaping the leadership skills Mr. Ford carried into office.

In 1930, on Thanksgiving Day, Gerald Ford captained his Grand Rapids, Michigan, South High School football team to the state championship. In celebration, the team formed the 30-30 Club for the 30 varsity lettermen that won the state title in 1930.

Every Thanksgiving Day from that point on, the 30-30 Club would meet in Grand Rapids. In the fall of 1974, when Mr. Ford was in the White House, he decided to have the meeting of the 30-30 Club at the people's house that Thanksgiving. He wanted his football teammates to join him, because he wanted around him people who he loved and trusted.

During his White House years, President Ford also prayed every night, as he had every night since he was a young boy, Proverbs 3:5–6, "Trust in the Lord with all thine heart, and lean not unto thine own understanding. In all thy ways acknowledge him, and he shall direct thy paths" (KJV). This verse, he told White House correspondent Trude Feldman, was a "steady compass and guide" for his life.

Consider what traditions you want to establish with your family and friends that relate to your walk with the Lord.

—ROXANNE ROBBINS

POINT AFTER

Look up the word *commitment* in the dictionary. Ask the Lord to help you commit to traditions that will help you grow as a Christian.

From the Playbook: Read Proverbs 3.

TOP 100 Kick/Punt Returners

NO. 1. MEL RENFRO 1963–1977 Dallas; 1964, Led NFL in punt return yards (418); 1964, Led NFL in kick return yards (1,017); 1969, Led NFL in interceptions (10); 1996, Inducted into HOF; 10 Pro Bowls; Punt return yards, 842; Kick return yards, 2,246.

FAITH QUOTE: *"Always when I go out to speak, a parent or young person will thank me for bringing God into their event."*

57. PONDER YOUR LIFE

Scrimmage Line:
Thinking through the effectiveness
of your life

"The heart of the wise is in the house of mourning."
ECCLESIASTES 7:4

Former Pro Bowl cornerback Aeneas Williams, who retired from the NFL in 2005, recalls stopping by a cemetery one day to ponder life. Ironically, his visit to that cemetery occurred just five days before Minnesota All-Pro offensive lineman Korey Stringer died from a heat stroke during a preseason workout in August 2001. Stringer was only 27.

FAST FACT:

Aeneas Williams played in 211 NFL games for the Cardinals and Rams during his career. After his career ended, he became the pastor of a church in Clayton, Missouri.

We all think we'll live to be 100. But truth be told, the average life expectancy today for a man is 75 years; for a woman, 80 years. And tragically, some die young, as Korey Stringer did. The Bible states that our time is fleeting—especially when compared to the time we will spend in eternity. On earth, we are not guaranteed any length of days, nor do we know either the time nor the day of our physical death.

In Psalm 39:4, David prays, "Show me, O Lord, my life's end and the number of my days; let me know how fleeting is my life." In fact, David went on to reveal this concept: "Each man's life is but a breath" (v. 5).

That's a good reason to, as Williams said after reflecting on his cemetery visit, "ponder your life today with the end in mind. It helps you make better decisions today because you live your life with an eternal perspective, not just day in and day out."

On a gravestone, there is a dash between the date of one's birth and the date of one's death. The truth is, there is really not much time between the two dates for any of us. That alone should make us ponder what we are doing for God's glory with that dash.

—MIKE SANDROLINI

POINT AFTER

What do you think God wants you to accomplish with your life? Are you either preparing to do that or already accomplishing it?

From the Playbook: Read Psalm 39:1–7.

Punt/Kick Returners

NO. 2. RICK UPCHURCH   1975–1983 Denver; 1977, Led NFL in punt return yards (653); 4 Pro Bowls; Punt return yards, 3,008; Kick return yards, 2,355.

FAITH QUOTE: *"God works through us in all kinds of ways. I want to tell kids that God is real, and He definitely won't fail you if you ask."*

58. NOT NORMAL

Scrimmage Line:
Pursuing Jesus passionately

"He appeared to me also, as to one abnormally born."
1 CORINTHIANS 15:8

Shaun Alexander never believed in aiming low. The MVP of the 2005 NFL season ran over and through defenders for 1,880 yards and a record 28 touchdowns to earn that honor.

Alexander had a goal to score 40 touchdowns in the 2006 season. Unfortunately, the start of that new NFL campaign did not go well for the gifted running back. After three games, he had just 187 total yards and an average of just 2.9 yards per carry.

FAST FACT:
Shaun Alexander had a career average of 4.3 yards per carry. That is just a touch better than the NFL's all-time leading rusher, Emmitt Smith (18,355 yards).

What's more, the NFL's MVP had a broken bone in his left foot. But Alexander, a strong believer in Jesus Christ, was not one to get down on himself. Instead he chose to press on. Unfortunately, he was never again able to amass the numbers he piled up in the 2005 season.

Something he said to reporters tells Alexander's story, "Every game I put unbelievable pressure on me to do things that are just not normal." For five NFL seasons, he did just that, rushing for more than 1,000 yards each year between 2001 and 2005. He scored 112 touchdowns in his career—the fourteenth best of all time. His 100 rushing TDs was seventh best ever.

The apostle Paul talked about being not normal too. He considered himself to be "abnormally born" (1 Corinthians 15:8) into faith in Jesus because he didn't, like other apostles, learn from Jesus while he was still alive on earth.

But like Shaun Alexander, Paul was also not normal in his uncompromising, determined goal to do great things in life. He chose to serve Jesus with all his heart, regardless of adversity. He also called others to join him in his passionate pursuit. "Hold firmly to the word I preached to you," he implored other believers. "Otherwise, you have believed in vain" (v. 2).

How are you "not normal" in your approach to living for Jesus? Where is your passionate pursuit of Him today?

—TOM FELTEN

POINT AFTER

Take out a sheet of paper and write down three "not normal" faith goals to pursue this week. Ask God to help you glorify Him as you desire to serve Jesus without compromise.

From the Playbook: Read 1 Corinthians 15:1–11.

TOP 100 Punt/Kick Returners

NO. 3. BILLY "WHITE SHOES" JOHNSON 1974–1988 Houston, Atlanta, Washington; 1975, Led NFL in punt return TDs (3); 3 Pro Bowls; Punt return yards, 3,317; Kick return yards, 2,941.

FAITH QUOTE: *"I want to be used to glorify God's name."*

59. LIVE WITH PURPOSE

*"Watch your life and doctrine . . . If you do, you
will save both yourself and your hearers."*
1 TIMOTHY 4:16

Norm Evans, offensive lineman for the Miami Dolphins
in the 1970s, is a man who has taken the apostle Paul's
words to Timothy to heart (1 Timothy 4:16). As a member of
the only NFL team to put together a perfect season all the way
through the Super Bowl—the 1972 Miami Dolphins—Norm
has had plenty of opportunities to be in the limelight and to
have countless "hearers."

As a Christian, however, Norm has made it a point to live
with purpose and to help others find their
purpose. He and his wife, Bobbe, head a ministry called Pro Athletes Outreach (PAO). This
Issaquah, Washington–based ministry helps
professional athletes interact with other pro
athletes regarding their faith in Jesus and their
daily walk with Him.

One way PAO does this is by bringing
together athletes from various sports to spend
five days each year in intense learning to help
one another deal with these two realities: They
are celebrities, and they are God's children. Intertwining the
two realities requires instruction and support.

Much of that instruction involves accountability. "Encourage one another daily," says Hebrews 3:13. If others you

FAST FACT:
*You can find out
more about the
work of PAO at
www.pao.org.
Danny and Jessica
Wuerffel are on
the Advisory
Council for PAO.*

trust are watching your life and doctrine closely, you will be forced to do the same. Otherwise, those you do not trust just might see the part of your life and doctrine that has been left unattended.

Norm has other accountability partners who help him to live a life worthy of God's calling—a life of purpose. I admire the steps he has taken to watch his own life and doctrine closely. It makes me consider how I might do the same.

Whether you're a pro athlete, a guy who plays H-O-R-S-E with the kids in the driveway, or a mom who chauffeurs the kids to soccer games, this accountability thing might be just what you need to help you live with a purpose.

—JESSICA WUERFFEL

POINT AFTER

What action steps can you take today to ensure that your life and doctrine are kept in check? Is there anyone who would be a good accountability partner to help you make those decisions?

From the Playbook: Read Ephesians 6:10–18.

NO. 1. STEVE TASKER   1985–1997 Houston, Buffalo; 7 Pro Bowls.

FAITH QUOTE: *"I feel that giving my testimony when I speak is something I need to do in return for all that God has given me."*

60. THE RIGHT DESIRE

*"Delight yourself in the Lord and he will give
you the desires of your heart."*

PSALM 37:4

For those of us who love sports, making a major professional team can seem like the ultimate dream. But for Michael Munoz, not being chosen in the 2005 NFL draft was simply a springboard to something better. He earned a master's degree in public administration, and after moving back to his native Ohio, won in his first run for political office—a trustee of a township near Cincinnati.

FAST FACT:

*Michael Munoz'
father, Anthony
Munoz, made
the Pro Bowl 11
times in his
career. He was
elected to the Pro
Football Hall of
Fame in 1998.*

NFL teams snubbed the Tennessee Volunteer All-American offensive tackle due to their concern about injuries. He took the rejection in stride. "I had fun playing football," said Munoz. "But I never found my identity playing football. Football isn't who I am."

Michael's peace about leaving football no doubt comes from the godly legacy his father bequeathed him. Anthony Munoz, a Hall-of-Fame offensive tackle for the Cincinnati Bengals, gave his life to Jesus when he was a collegiate standout struggling with injuries. Calling Michael's rejection by the NFL "a divine intervention," the elder Munoz said, "One door was closed and there's four or five other doors being opened." Michael and Anthony Munoz are teaching us about godly priorities and valuing eternal things over what is dead and dying.

A great songwriter once sang about God giving us "the desires of [our] heart" (Psalm 37:4). But the prerequisite to getting our desires is finding our joy and delight in God himself. If we are truly prioritizing our lives around what matters, we'll want what God wants.

Athletic competition is a gift from God. But making a god out of a sport puts us in competition with God's desires. The more important consideration for all of us—athletes or not—is this: Do I want what God wants?

—TIM GUSTAFSON

POINT AFTER

What are your top five priorities? What does this say about you and your relationship to God? How do you react when you lose something that you wanted badly? Have you given your desires to God?

From the Playbook: Read Psalm 37:1–11.

NO. 2. BILL BATES 1983–1997 Dallas; 1 Pro Bowl; Fumble recoveries, career: 7.

FAITH QUOTE: *"God put me here to make a difference in the lives of others, and I hope, lead them to the Lord."*

61. GIVE IT UP!

*"Offer your bodies as living sacrifices,
holy and pleasing to God."*

ROMANS 12:1

What's the first thing that comes to your mind when you hear the word *surrender*? For me, it is a white flag—a symbol of giving up. You know what? That is how the world wants us to view surrender—as a weakness, as an act of defeat and sorrow.

But Christ says just the opposite. In His vocabulary, surrender is essential. It is the positive act of dying to self every day and coming into full submission to the Father. That is definitely not about giving up.

FAST FACT:

You can read about Ben's gospel recording career at www.benutecht.com.

The apostle Paul had this down! In Acts 20:24, he says, "I consider my life worth nothing to me, if only I may finish the race and complete the task the Lord Jesus has given me—the task of testifying to the gospel of God's grace." Paul didn't care what hardships came his way, because he was in a constant state of surrender.

Ask yourself, "Have I truly surrendered all that I am and all that I have to this God I serve?" Through my suffering with numerous injuries during my college football career, Christ asked me this question, and He opened my eyes to the power of surrender. He brought me out of darkness into the light by giving me an opportunity to play in the NFL.

When I began playing for the Indianapolis Colts—against really huge odds, I tried to submit all that I was to Him. Meanwhile, my identity was not as a professional football player, but as a Christian.

Each day I wake up, roll out of bed onto my knees, and pray a prayer of surrender. I encourage you to make this a daily process. It will ensure that Christ is the ultimate leader of your day and of your life. He wants everything, so give it to Him. Then watch what He does with you!

—BEN UTECHT

POINT AFTER

What are three things you need to surrender to God today? Make a checklist to help you keep track of your commitment.

From the Playbook: Read Romans 12:1–8.

TOP 100 Defensive Linemen

NO. 1. REGGIE WHITE 1985–2000 Philadelphia, Green Bay, Carolina; 1987, 1988 Led NFL in sacks (21, 18); 13 Pro Bowls; 2006, Inducted into the HOF; 1987, 1988, NFL Defensive Player of the Year; 1991, Bart Starr Award; Career sacks, 198. Date of death: December 26, 2004.

FAITH QUOTE: *"Other than my relationship with Jesus, Sara [my wife] is the most important person in my life."*

62. TAKING RISKS

Scrimmage Line:
Using your potential for God's glory

"Well done, good and faithful servant!"
MATTHEW 25:21

Each April hundreds of collegiate football players from around the country hope that a team will take a chance and make them one of their picks in the annual NFL Draft. They all want to be one of the 256 players the NFL thinks is worthy of a pick in the draft.

FAST FACT:

The first No. 1 pick in the NFL draft was Heisman Trophy winner Jay Berwanger of the University of Chicago in 1936. Some others: O. J. Simpson, Terry Bradshaw, Troy Aikman, Michael Vick, and Eli Manning.

No matter how high the pick, drafting players out of college is a risky business. A team could score big with the No. 1 overall pick and take a player of the caliber of John Elway (1983) or Peyton Manning (1998). On the other hand, a team could come up short with the No. 1 pick and draft a player like Bo Jackson (Tampa Bay, 1986), who opted to play professional baseball or Tim Couch (Cleveland, 1999), who played only five seasons and never cracked the Top 10 in any quarterback category.

Drafting players is a lot like taking risks in everyday life. It can turn out good, or just about anything can go wrong. But that is no excuse to sit back and play it safe.

Jesus once told a story about the dangers of playing it safe (Matthew 25:14–30). Before taking a long journey, a master entrusted three of his servants with three different sums of money. When he returned, the master found that two of the servants faithfully put the money to work despite the risks involved. They doubled the master's money and earned his highest praise and reward. The third servant, however, refused to take a risk and hid the money in the ground. And it didn't go so well for him (vv. 26–30).

Life is filled with risk and uncertainty, but real loss comes when we don't use what God has given us to its fullest potential.

—JEFF OLSON

POINT AFTER

Where is God calling you to stop playing it safe?

For Further Study: Go to www.discoveryseries.org and search for the booklet *Why in the World Am I Here?*

TOP 100
Defensive Linemen

NO. 2. BOB LILLY   1961–1974 Dallas; 1963, Led NFL with longest fumble return (42 yards); 11 Pro Bowls; 1980, Inducted into the HOF.

FAITH QUOTE: *"I rededicated my life to the Lord, and that started to change my perspective on some things."*

63. TOUGH ENOUGH

"Train yourself to be godly."
1 TIMOTHY 4:7

Did you hear the one about the pro football team that got two days off with full pay because their coach was a meanie?

In 2006 the Detroit Lions were forced to take two days off from supervised drills because the team's new head coach, Rod Marinelli, conducted an April mini-camp that was "too physical."

FAST FACT:
Rod Marinelli lasted three years with the Lions, compiling a record of 10-38. He then moved on to be an assistant coach with the Chicago Bears.

The NFL Players Association and the NFL Management Council came down on Marinelli and his staff due to his strenuous workouts. An interesting observation about this account is the fact that the *players* complained that Rod's road to conditioning was over the line. But these are players whose team had gone a combined 21-59 over the previous five NFL seasons! You would think they might be ready for some serious effort to change their performance.

No. They complained and ended up with some extra free time. It is no wonder, then, that Marinelli failed in his efforts to turn around a franchise that hadn't won a playoff game since the 1991–1992 season.

From a spiritual perspective, are you winning or is this season of life another disappointing one? If things aren't going well, it may be that your "workouts" simply aren't tough enough.

In 1 Timothy 4 the apostle Paul told his understudy Timothy to get serious about his spiritual maturity. "Train yourself to be godly," he told his charge. "For physical training is of some value, but godliness has value for all things" (vv. 7–8).

Two words come to mind in considering Paul's instruction—*discipline* and *effort*. If you don't include these qualities in your spiritual training, you're headed nowhere. Get going with that memorization, prayer, and reading of the Word. Don't worry, you won't ever be guilty of working too hard at this. But you will get tougher spiritually. Are you tough enough?

—TOM FELTEN

POINT AFTER

Write down a spiritual-disciplines plan for this week. Strive to follow it by praying to God for strength and by seeking accountability with a godly friend.

From the Playbook: Read 1 Timothy 4:1–10.

TOP 100 Defensive Linemen

NO. 3. BILL GLASS   1958–1968 Detroit, Cleveland; 4 Pro Bowls; President, Bill Glass Ministries.

FAITH QUOTE: *"Like Paul the apostle, I have found that whatsoever state I am in, therewith to be content."*

64. FLEETING FAME AND ETERNAL GLORY

*"You will receive the crown of glory
that will never fade away."*

1 PETER 5:4

Quick! Who were the heroes of Super Bowl I? If you mention Bart Starr, quarterback of the winning Green Bay Packers, congratulations. But who was Starr's favorite receiver on January 15, 1967?

In winning MVP honors as the Packers defeated the Kansas City Chiefs 35-14, Starr completed only 17 of 32 passes. But seven of those tosses were snagged by Max McGee, a backup receiver who had caught only four passes during the regular season. McGee, subbing for the ailing Boyd Dowler, totaled 138 receiving yards and two touchdowns. Elijah Pitts added two rushing TDs. Not exactly household names.

Each year in early February, football fans both rabid and sporadic gather around the TV to see the NFL's two best teams battle it out. And each time the Roman numeral game arrives, we have no idea what unlikely heroes will emerge. But one thing is clear. They will rise to prominence only for a brief moment and then recede into the shadows of football lore.

FAST FACT:

Each member of the 1967 Packers took home a $15,000 check—at that time the largest prize ever for a team championship. Kansas City received $7,500. By SB XLIII, the winner's share had climbed to $83,000.

Most of us can only dream of Super Bowl stardom. But we all have the hope of something infinitely superior to MVP trophies and championship rings. The apostle Peter wrote of "an inheritance that can never perish, spoil or fade" (1 Peter 1:4). That rich inheritance grows out of our faith in Jesus, a faith that is more precious than gold (vv. 6–7).

Peter's co-disciple John wrote of the fleeting nature of the things this world values. "The world and its desires pass away," John said, "but the man who does the will of God lives forever" (1 John 2:17).

Next time the Super Bowl comes around, enjoy it and its surprising heroes. (I know I will.) But never lose sight of the things that count forever.

—Tim Gustafson

POINT AFTER

Do you have the faith that Peter speaks of (1 Peter 1:7)? Who is the object of your faith? Is it Jesus? If not, why not ask Him to forgive you and become Lord of your life today?

From the Playbook: Read 1 Peter 1:3–9.

TOP 100 Defensive Linemen

NO. 4. MICHAEL SINCLAIR 1992–2002 Seattle, Philadelphia; 1998, Led NFL in sacks (16.5); 3 Pro Bowls.

FAITH QUOTE: *"God has always provided for me and my family."*

65. THE ULTIMATE VICTORY

"Thanks be to God! He gives us the victory through our Lord Jesus Christ."

1 CORINTHIANS 15:57

September 24, 1994. Ann Arbor, Michigan. Fifteen seconds left in the game, 85 yards to cover.

Kordell Stewart, quarterback for the University of Colorado, stares into the face of the Michigan Stadium scoreboard, which displays a 26-21 Michigan lead over the Buffaloes.

FAST FACT:
Colorado's stunning 1994 victory came in front of 106,427 fans at Michigan Stadium.

After a couple of quick hits, Stewart has advanced the Buffaloes to the Colorado 36-yard line, and now there are just six seconds left. The Michigan fans get ready to celebrate a win of the fourth-ranked Wolverines over the seventh-rated Buffs.

What happened next was unbelievable. Stewart stepped back, scrambled to avoid a Wolverine defender, then threw the ball as far as he could. The pass reached the goal line—75 yards away. It was tipped by a couple of Colorado players, and then it was swallowed up by Michigan-native-turned-CU-receiver Michael Westbrook, who fell to the turf in the end zone with a miraculous 64-yard, game-winning touchdown pass for the visitors.

"For me personally," Colorado coach Bill McCartney said of the remarkable finish, "this is the ultimate victory."

McCartney is a Christian, so we can surmise that he was speaking only about football—since he understands the true ultimate victory.

In 1 Corinthians 15, we read about *that* victory. Through His death on the cross, our Lord and Savior gives us victory over sin and ultimately over separation from Him in heaven. Not even the huge scoreboard at Cowboys Stadium in Dallas is big enough to display that kind of win!

Without Jesus, we were destined for death, but because of Jesus' ultimate sacrifice, He gives us the biggest win of them all—salvation and the promise of spending eternity with our Lord in heaven. Now, that is the ultimate victory!

—JEFF ARNOLD

POINT AFTER

Take a second to consider what obstacle you're facing right now. Just remember, you don't need a miracle finish to overcome it. Take it to Jesus; ask Him to show you how to beat the opponent you're facing. He's faithful—and in the end, that's all that matters.

From the Playbook: Read 1 Corinthians 15.

TOP 100 Defensive Linemen

NO. 5. TOMMIE HARRIS   2004– Chicago; 3 Pro Bowls.

FAITH QUOTE: *"The main thing I found is that you stay plugged in to the Lord. Because anything that comes unplugged loses its power."*

66. SUPER BOWL LXVI

"He commanded us to preach to the people."
ACTS 10:42

Are you ready for Super Bowl LXVI?
Wait a second, you're thinking. If you have your Roman numerals right, Super Bowl LXVI won't be played until 2032. True, but during a Super Bowl party at First Baptist Church in Colleyville, Texas, in February 2006, LXVI (66) young people received Jesus Christ as Savior.

FAST FACT:

Jerome Bettis gained 43 yards on 14 carries for the Steelers in Super Bowl XL, which was played in his hometown of Detroit. He retired from the NFL after that game.

Sure, they got to see the "Bus," Jerome Bettis, do his stuff—helping his team to a 21-10 Pittsburgh Steelers victory over the Seattle Seahawks in Super Bowl XL. But the 400 youth attending the party also took in a half-time presentation of God's plan of salvation presented by the *Power to Win* folks.

During the third quarter, ten of the new believers in Jesus chose to be baptized, and the following weekend some attended a "Disciple Now" conference.

LXVI—now *that's* a Super Bowl number to get excited about!

Whether we are watching the Big Game with friends, helping a neighbor rake leaves, or working out at the local gym—all of these opportunities are openings for us to live out our faith in Jesus. We can use many of the events of life to present the good news.

The apostle Peter knew what to do when he was invited to the house of Cornelius, a centurion in the Italian Regiment. As he stood before the man's assembled guests, he opened his mouth and told them of the "good news of peace through Jesus Christ" (Acts 10:36).

Why did he do this? Because Jesus had told him to "preach to the people . . . that everyone who believes in him receives forgiveness of sins" (vv. 42–43).

Like Peter and like the Colleyville church, let's find ways to use the events of life to "preach" Christ!

—TOM FELTEN

POINT AFTER

Check out your calendar and look for events of this week that will allow you to share Jesus—by word and action—with others in attendance. Highlight a couple of the events and pray for the opportunity to "preach to the people."

From the Playbook: Read Acts 10:25–43.

Top 100 Defensive Linemen

NO. 6. KEVIN CARTER 1995–2008 St. Louis, Tennessee, Miami, Tampa Bay; 1999, Led NFL in sacks; 2 Pro Bowls.

FAITH QUOTE: *"God's grace and His love are sufficient for my life."*

67. THE BIG SWITCH

"Therefore, if anyone is in Christ, he is a new creation."

2 CORINTHIANS 5:17

In May 1983, after completing my college education at the University of South Carolina, I attended my first NFL mini-camp. The Atlanta Falcons had drafted me in the third round. During these spring activities, coaches and players focus on noncontact skills in preparation for the opening of training camp in July.

FAST FACT:

The average weight for an NFL lineman in 1977 was approximately 255 pounds. By 2007, that average had climbed to well over 300 pounds.

As I walked through the Falcons' locker room for the first time, I noticed a pair of large football shoes hanging from a player's locker. The shoes belonged to a 293-pound, 6' 7" offensive tackle Brett Miller. I was awestruck by the size of this man.

At times, I wished I could get inside another football player's huge body and just borrow it for a while—just to see what it would be like. That's what happened, kind of, in the movie *Freaky Friday* when a mother and daughter temporarily switch bodies. Chaos ensued, but they did find out some important things about the other person.

When we begin a relationship with Christ, God allows us to keep our original body. However, he does make a switch. He removes our old life and replaces it with His new life in our same body. Second Corinthians 5:17 reads, "Therefore, if anyone is in Christ, he is a new creation; the old has gone, the new has come!"

As Christians, our true inner person is totally new and complete in Christ. Our thinking, however, must continue to be renewed. And our body remains the same old one—one we have to take good care of until our perfect, super body is issued to us in heaven.

Let's live like the creations we are—with hearts that are dedicated to loving God and serving others.

—ANDREW PROVENCE

POINT AFTER

Check out a Bible study website and take a look at the phrase "in Christ" throughout the New Testament.

From the Playbook: Read Romans 6:3–8.

Defensive Linemen

NO. 7. AARON KAMPMAN   2002– Green Bay; 2 Pro Bowls; 2006, Recorded 15.5 sacks (second in NFL).

FAITH QUOTE: *"It's a good thing to have other guys around you who are committed to being used by the Lord."*

68. ME, A MINISTER?

*"All this is from God, who . . . gave us
the ministry of reconciliation."*

2 CORINTHIANS 5:18

Reggie White was an ordained minister who dominated opponents on the football field. That rather rare combination led to the nickname "Minister of Defense" while he played his college football at the University of Tennessee. The nickname stayed with him through the legendary defensive lineman's NFL career with the Philadelphia Eagles, Green Bay Packers, and Carolina Panthers.

FAST FACT:
President Gerald R. Ford died two years to the day after Reggie White died. In 1935, Ford was offered a contract with the Green Bay Packers, the team with whom White won the Super Bowl in 1997.

When he retired, he was second on the NFL's all-time sack list with 198 in his career. Only Buffalo Bills star Bruce Smith was ahead of Reggie. (And remember this, White began his pro career in the now-defunct USFL with the Memphis Showboats, so his sack total is missing two full seasons of NFL football.)

In 2006, Reggie, who died unexpectedly on December 26, 2004, was elected posthumously into the Pro Football Hall of Fame in Canton, Ohio.

As followers of Jesus Christ, you and I also have been given a role that closely matches White's well-known moniker. In his second letter to the church in Corinth, the apostle Paul reveals our responsibility. For those of us who are "in Christ," those who have a relationship with Jesus, God has given us the ministry of reconciliation. Simply put, God is making His appeal to a dying world through you and me! He uses His followers to spread the message of forgiveness and reconciliation that can only be found through a personal relationship with God through Jesus Christ.

If you are a Christ-follower, God has given you, just as he gave Reggie White, the great responsibility of being a minister. You truly are a "Minister of Reconciliation."

—ROB BENTZ

POINT AFTER

Pray for three people in your life who are not believers. Ask God to let you faithfully communicate the message of reconciliation to God through Jesus to them this week.

From the Playbook: Read and meditate on 2 Corinthians 5:11–21.

TOP 100 Defensive Linemen

NO. 8. LUTHER ELLISS   1995–2004 Detroit, Denver; 2 Pro Bowls; 29 career sacks.

FAITH QUOTE: *"The hunger I have is for Christ—to know who He is. To know the Bible from Genesis to Revelation."*

69. MY BELOVED

*"Dear friends, let us love one another,
for love comes from God."*

1 JOHN 4:7

I was married on July 15, 2006. Wow, what an amazing experience! Talk about feeling the presence of God! It was also special because my father, Jeff Utecht, a United Methodist minister, performed the ceremony as I married my college sweetheart, Karyn Stordahl.

God is so good, and through my relationship with Karyn, He has opened my eyes and heart to the beauty and importance of loving others. As 1 John indicates, "God is love" and when we love others, we are truly reflecting God.

FAST FACT:
Ben and Kara welcomed their first child, Elleora Grace, on March 1, 2009.

As I have walked through the first few years of this lifelong union with my wife Karyn, I realize that the only way it will work is if I strive to love her the way Christ loves me: unconditionally. You see, our whole faith revolves around a divine relationship.

Hmmm. I wonder if God was trying to tell us something! Yes, relationships are incredibly important. How we pour out our love on others determines the success of those relationships.

So, if you ever find it difficult to love someone—a teammate, an opponent, a coach, your spouse, a friend, or a family member, look to the One who created love. Remember Jesus' sacrifice, and make the choice to go out and demonstrate that kind of selfless love to everyone you encounter.

Do this and your relationships will be a success. Christ gave His life as a symbol of love—let us take that love and change the world.

—BEN UTECHT

POINT AFTER

How important is love to you? Do you try to get through life without spending much time considering how you should love the people in your life? Seek ways to love them as God loves you.

From the Playbook: Read 1 John 4:7–12.

Defensive Linemen

NO. 9. GREG ELLIS 1998–2009 Dallas, Oakland; 2007, NFL Comeback Player of the Year; 1 Pro Bowl; 84 career sacks.

FAITH QUOTE: *"True leadership is godly leadership and godly leadership is the best leadership."*

70. TAKE A STAND

"Put on the full armor of God."
EPHESIANS 6:11

In Daniel 5 we learn of a king who fell from glory because of pride. Daniel said to him, "You his son, O Belshazzar, have not humbled yourself" (v. 22).

Despite knowing God's commands (v. 22), Belshazzar chose to worship himself instead of God (v. 23). His downfall was ugly. In fact, before the night described in this story was over, Belshazzar's kingdom was defeated, and his city was overrun by the Persians.

Several years ago, I was overseeing the media relations for the Athletes in Action Bart Starr Award. The award is given each year on the day before the Super Bowl to an NFL player who AIA feels best exemplifies character at home and in the community. On this particular year, a well-known Atlanta Falcons player received the award. On that Saturday morning, he stood before a large audience accepting the award and testifying of his relationship with Jesus Christ.

My ministry colleagues and I were shocked a few hours later to learn that on that same night, on the eve of playing in the Super Bowl and mere hours after receiving an award for good character, the Bart Starr Award winner was arrested for soliciting a prostitute. His actions were costly. His reputation

FAST FACT:
Among the winners of the Bart Starr Award are LaDainian Tomlinson, Chargers; Warrick Dunn, Bucs; Curtis Martin, Jets; and Derrick Brooks, Bucs.

and Christian testimony were severely damaged. He brought shame and hurt to his wife and family. And his behavior appeared to have a negative influence on his team's performance in the Super Bowl the next day.

God wants us to be used for holy purposes. Satan wants us to be used for unholy purposes. That's the daily battle we are all involved in.

Ephesians 6:11 tell us to "Put on the full armor of God so that you can take your stand against the devil's schemes."

Are you wearing your armor? You must if you want to take a stand—and not get knocked down.

—ROXANNE ROBBINS

POINT AFTER

List the components of the "armor" found in Ephesians 6.

From the Playbook: Read Ephesians 6.

Defensive Linemen

NO. 10. RUSSELL MARYLAND 1991–2000 Dallas, Oakland, Green Bay; 1 Pro Bowl; 24.5 career sacks.

FAITH QUOTE: *"All the things I've accomplished in football and in academics couldn't have been accomplished if it weren't for my relationship with the Lord Jesus Christ."*

71. SEEING IS BELIEVING

*"You are the God who performs miracles;
you display your power among the peoples."*

PSALM 77:14

The Music City Miracle of January 8, 2000, remains a defining moment in the annals of Tennessee Titans football lore. Trailing the Buffalo Bills 16-15 with 16 seconds to play in an opening-round AFC playoff game, the Titans were set to receive the kickoff when Titans coach Jeff Fisher called for a play he called the Home Run Throwback. What happened next was one of the most incredible events in NFL history.

The Titans' Lorenzo Neal received the kick at his own 25-yard line and handed the ball to tight end Frank Wycheck. As the Bills' defenders barreled toward Wycheck, he turned and threw the ball laterally across the field to waiting wide receiver Kevin Dyson. He reached down and grabbed the ball at his shoe tops and took off downfield. A surprised Bills defense couldn't catch him, and Dyson scampered 75 yards for a game-winning touchdown. That remarkable play paved the way for the Titans' Super Bowl run.

FAST FACT:

In the closing seconds of the Super Bowl against the St. Louis Rams, Mike Jones tackled the Titans' Kevin Dyson one yard short of a game-winning touchdown.

While there is no doubt that this was a pretty cool play, it was not, as the common appellation suggests, a miracle.

A miracle is something only God could do—things such as Jesus making the blind see, allowing the lame to walk, and turning a few loaves of bread and a couple fish into enough food to feed 5,000 people. Let the Titans try that!

In Psalm 77, we learn that God is partially defined through his ability to do miracles, which displays His power (v. 14). But God's ability for miracles isn't limited to the past. God does things in our lives that we think are impossible. How many times has God worked in your life and you respond: "Only God can do that!" God's power is unlimited, and He is able to do anything. Call on Him and then sit back and watch what He chooses to do.

—JEFF ARNOLD

POINT AFTER

Maybe you're dealing with something that requires God's power. If so, tell Jesus about it and ask that He reveal His power to you in your situation. Then all He requires is that you trust Him for the results.

From the Playbook: Read Psalm 77.

NO. 1. MIKE SINGLETARY   1981–1992 Chicago; 1988, Defensive Player of the Year; 1990, NFL Man of the Year; 1990, Bart Starr Award; 1998, Inducted into HOF; 10 Pro Bowls.

FAITH QUOTE: *"Understand that your body is the temple of Jesus Christ. Understand that you are loved. Understand the price that has been paid for you by Jesus."*

72. HOW TO LOVE BY FAITH

Scrimmage Line:
Answering God's call for service

"Should I not be concerned about that great city?"
JONAH 4:11

In sports terms, it would be like Michigan vs. Ohio State, Miami vs. FSU, or Notre Dame vs. USC. Jonah's assignment from God is something like me, the Miami chaplain, being asked to do chapel for Florida State on game day. The more realistic comparison might be something like asking an Orthodox Jewish rabbi to go tell Hitler that God loves him and offers a wonderful plan for his life.

God had a purpose for Jonah, but that purpose meant he would have to do a very difficult job.

As He did with Jonah, God calls us to serve. He has a purpose for our lives. He disciplines us because He loves us. He rescues us when our disobedience threatens our life and others we are called to help. He gives us a second chance. He is "gracious and compassionate . . . , slow to anger and abounding in love, a God who relents from sending calamity" (Jonah 4:2).

He is a God who provides a vine for our comfort. Then he removes the vine so we can identify with the pain of those who live without His comfort and provision (see Jonah 4:6–8). God wanted Jonah to have His heart. He wanted Jonah to care about the things He cares about—to love the people He loves. He wanted Jonah then, and you and me now, to give our lives for His purpose.

What about you? Are you living your life for a purpose? Are you seeking clear guidance from God about how He wants you to serve Him in love and by faith?

Do you have the heart of God for people in the world who don't know Him? It's a tough job, but it's what God calls us to do.

—STEVE DEBARDELABEN

POINT AFTER

When was the last time you took it upon yourself to do the tough job of sharing the gospel? Is that part of the purpose for your life?

From the Playbook: Read Jonah 4.

Linebackers

NO. 2. RANDY GRADISHAR 1974–1983 Denver; 1978, Defensive Player of the Year; 7 Pro Bowls.

FAITH QUOTE: *"I've been wanting and desiring to know more of God and to strengthen my faith—more experiencing God and a more personal relationship with Him."*

73. LASTING SATISFACTION

*"[God] anointed us, set his seal of ownership on us, . . .
guaranteeing what is to come."*

2 CORINTHIANS 1:21–22

Prior to coaching in the NFL, Dave Wannstedt spent three
years as the University of Miami defensive coordinator.
While Wannstedt was with the team, the Hurricanes went
34-2 (.944) and won the national championship in 1987.

FAST FACT:

*Dave Wannstedt
played tackle at
Pitt, where he
blocked for Heis-
man Trophy win-
ner Tony Dorsett.
Later, he became
the head coach at
his alma mater.*

From Miami, Wannstedt journeyed with head
coach Jimmy Johnson to Dallas where they
took over the coaching chores for the Cowboys.
Just three years later, the Chicago Bears gave
Wannstedt his first head coaching position. It
was a few weeks into his career with the Bears
that I had the opportunity to do an exclusive
interview with the coach.

Wannstedt told me that up to that point the
highlight of his football career had been when
the Hurricanes won the national championship. Yet he said that this experience also led
him to the lowest point of his life.

"I had dreamed of winning the national championship for
many years," Wannstedt told me. "When it actually happened,
I was ecstatic. But just two days later, I felt the heaviest letdown I had ever experienced."

Wannstedt called Miami team chaplain Steve DeBardelaben and said he needed to meet with him right away. Dave

explained to Steve that he had expected the championship to fill him with permanent satisfaction, but instead the thrill of winning provided merely temporary happiness. Shortly after the elation, he once again felt empty.

It was at that point that Wannstedt, through DeBardelaben's careful and clear guidance, recognized that only Jesus Christ could permanently fill the void in his heart. Wannstedt's post-national championship letdown led him to lasting security in Christ.

Have you ever been where Coach Wannstedt was? Have you ever achieved an important life goal—only to discover that its glory faded quickly?

If so, you need lasting satisfaction. That's what you can have when you trust Jesus Christ, the One who died for you to give you eternal life.

—ROXANNE ROBBINS

POINT AFTER

How has a disappointment in your life helped you grow closer to Christ?

From the Playbook: Read 2 Corinthians 1.

TOP 100 Linebackers

NO. 3. CHRIS SPIELMAN 1988–1997 Detroit, Buffalo; Inducted into College Football Hall of Fame, 2009; 4 Pro Bowls; Career tackles, 1,181.

FAITH QUOTE: *Referring to the death of his wife, Stephanie, who died of cancer in 2009: "You either run to God or away from God through trials and tribulations."*

74. JUST "PLANE" PRAYER

"The Lord will fight for you; you need only to be still."

EXODUS 14:14

Fred Taylor, who was enjoying his offseason while a member of the Jacksonville Jaguars, had quite a scare. He and fellow NFL players Samari Rolle and Lito Sheppard, along with their wives, were returning from a safari in South Africa when a heart-stopping event took place—but it had nothing to do with seeing fierce mammals up close and personal.

No, the scary part of the story began when Fred and his friends were flying back to their hotel in a single-propeller plane. While they were cruising at 6,000 feet, suddenly the door of the craft flew open!

"I thought that was it," Fred said. "I put my head down and started praying."

Fortunately, the pilot was able to land the plane—on a wing and some prayers!

I don't know Fred Taylor's spiritual state, but it is interesting to note his first reaction when he thought the plane was going down. He *prayed*.

When the Israelites thought they were about to get mowed down by Pharaoh's army—pinned against the Red Sea—they "cried out to the Lord" (Exodus 14:10). Sadly, however, they doubted God's leading and protection.

Moses had to remind the people that "The Lord will fight for you; you need only to be still" (v. 14). And that's exactly what happened—God allowed Israel to pass through the Red Sea on dry land while Pharaoh's entire army was wiped out when the Lord caused the waters to crash in on them.

When you face sudden events that threaten you, what is your first reaction? It *is* good to call out to God in prayer. But a deeper issue is *trusting* God—remaining still—and allowing Him to reveal His power.

Just plain prayer can't compete with prayer that is based on a real faith in God!

—TOM FELTEN

POINT AFTER

Think about your reactions to some of the sudden, scary situations that you have faced. What will it take for you to respond to the next one with real trust in God and prayers that reflect that trust? Pray today for a still, unshakable faith that is prepared for tomorrow's troubles.

From the Playbook: Read Exodus 14:10–28.

Top 100 Linebackers

NO. 4. DERRICK BROOKS 1995–2008 Tampa Bay; 2000, NFL Man of the Year; 2002, NFL Defensive Player of the Year; 2003, Bart Starr Award; 11 Pro Bowls.

FAITH QUOTE: *Upon being named Defensive Player of the Year: "The fraternity I want to be a part of . . . is in heaven. I tell people all the time these things are great, but the award I'm striving for is to spend eternity with God." While at Florida State, he says he "got down on my knees and accepted Jesus as my Lord and Savior and asked Him to forgive my sins."*

75. WORTHLESS IDOLS

Scrimmage Line:
Putting God before all else

"He who conceals his sins does not prosper."
PROVERBS 28:13

The Old Testament prophet Jonah brought trouble on himself and those closest to him with his disobedience. His resistance to the Holy Spirit brought severe discipline into his life. He was thrown into the sea without hope, but the God of hope provided a great fish to rescue him.

Jonah prayed to the Lord and said, "In my distress I called to the Lord, and he answered me . . . When my life was ebbing away, I remembered you, Lord" (Jonah 2:2–7). He knew where to turn in time of need. And he knew what would not help. He observed: "Those who cling to worthless idols forfeit the grace that could be theirs" (v. 8).

FAST FACT:

Steve DeBardelaben is a chaplain with Athletes in Action. To read about the work of Athletes in Action and its chaplains, go to athletesinaction .com.

In the mid-90s a head coach at Miami felt the need for a coaching change on his staff. A friend of mine became a candidate for the job. We jogged and prayed and talked about how great it would be for him to get that position. Several days passed and there was no word from the decision-maker in Miami. My friend became angry and frustrated with the circumstance.

We jogged and prayed and talked some more, and the Lord seemed to be telling my friend, "The dream is a good one. But it is not good if it is the source of your peace and personal significance. Put me and my will above everything in your life. That job can be a great servant, but it is a terrible master."

My friend let go of what could have been a worthless idol. He sought the Lord with his whole heart instead of the job. Later that day he got a call, interviewed for the job, and became a significant part of the success of that team.

Are you clinging to any worthless idols? Let go. Depend completely on the one true God—and trust Him with the results.

—STEVE DeBARDELABEN

POINT AFTER

Is there something you value so much it is stopping you from being obedient to God? Would it help your relationship with God to let go of it and depend totally on Him?

From the Playbook: Read Jonah 2.

Linebackers

NO. 5. HARDY NICKERSON 1987–2002 Pittsburgh, Tampa Bay, Jacksonville, Green Bay; 5 Pro Bowls.

FAITH QUOTE: *"I've been blessed to be on the field and have a platform. I want to use this platform to glorify God and help people."*

76. DON'T OUT-KICK THE COVERAGE

*"I will say of the Lord, 'He is my refuge
and my fortress, my God.'"*

PSALM 91:2

Punting is an important part of football. When backed up deep on their side of the field, successful teams learn to kick the ball away on fourth down and use a well-placed kick to help them get better field position.

FAST FACT:

The most punts in a season by an NFL team is 116 by the 2002 Houston Texans. The fewest? The San Diego Chargers punted just 23 times in 1982.

It may seem that punting is one of the easiest things to do in football. The reality is that there is a lot that goes into this skill. It's not simply a matter of booting the ball downfield as far as possible. Sure, it's great when a punter gets a good foot into it. Certainly, coaches don't want their punter to shank one off the side of his foot. But one of the things that drives special-teams coaches crazy is the punter who out-kicks his coverage. Kicking the ball past the area a punter's teammates can cover could turn into a big play for the opposition.

Living the Christian life requires staying within our coverage too—spiritual coverage. It's generally not wise, for example, to start your day or embark on a serious venture without asking for God's protection. It is especially unwise to take action in a difficult "fourth down" type of life situation without praying for God's safety. Staying within your spiritual coverage is not only an important part of walking with God but it's also a part of guarding yourself against a dangerous enemy who poses a real threat to you. Think David and Goliath, if you need an example. Imagine what would have happened had David gone after the Big Dude without God's protection and help.

Don't out-kick your coverage. Respond to life in light of Jesus' warning that there is a real enemy who will do whatever he can to "steal and kill and destroy" the life we can have in our Lord (John 10:10). Stay in God's protected zone.

—JEFF OLSON

POINT AFTER

Read Ephesians 6:11–17 and list five specific ways these verses can help you avoid the danger of "out-kicking your coverage."

For Further Study: Search for the Discovery Series booklet *What in the World Is Satan Doing?* at www.discoveryseries.org.

TOP 100 Linebackers

NO 6. JOHN OFFERDAHL 1986–1993 Miami; 5 Pro Bowls.

FAITH QUOTE: *"I want people to know when they hear my name that here's a guy who lives a Christian life."*

77. LESSONS FROM FANTASY FOOTBALL

"When he asks, he must believe and not doubt."

JAMES 1:6

My church's men's ministry started a fantasy football league. When it first began, I had never played before, so I actually knew nothing about it. It seemed like a great way to connect with other men, so I joined the league.

Fantasy football has been an eye-opener in several ways. First, it can be addictive. This may be what's driving a rapidly growing fantasy sports industry. Second, it has incited emotions that I have not felt since I was an active NFL player. Third, it has created an uncomfortable experience of double-mindedness.

I have found myself wanting my fantasy players to do well, even if they are playing against my "real life" favorite teams. I have attempted to keep some Atlanta Falcons and Denver Broncos (my former "real life" teams) fantasy players on my team.

In the real world (vs. fantasy), when opposing players do well against our team, it hurts our team. We can't cheer for players on team "A" and be a loyal fan of team "B."

James warns us against this kind of double-mindedness in the real world. James 1:8 states that we become "unstable" in all we do. And he says that a person like that won't have an effective prayer life.

Where can the wisdom James 1 talks about be found in fantasy sports? Well, I have connected more with the men in the church (including my son). Also, it's been sobering to keep track of the overwhelming number of injuries during an NFL season. It is an opportunity to pray for those players and their families.

And most important, it reminds me not to be double-minded in my prayer life. The reality of it is that we must "believe and not doubt" (v. 6) if we want to pray God's way.

—ANDREW PROVENCE

POINT AFTER

How are you connecting with others? Are you seeking healthy relationships? Ask the Lord for wisdom in how to do this.

From the Playbook: Read James 1:1–8.

TOP 100 Linebackers

NO. 7. BRYCE PAUP 1990–2000 Green Bay, Buffalo, Jacksonville, Minnesota; 1995, Led NFL in sacks (17.5); 4 Pro Bowls.

FAITH QUOTE: "When you stay in the Word of God, you stay focused on God."

78. FORWARD PASS

*"Then [Moses] laid his hands on [Joshua]
and commissioned him."*

NUMBERS 27:23

On January 12, back in 1906, the football rules committee was busy legalizing the forward pass! Yes, you read that right. And it was none other than Georgia Tech's football coach John Heisman who convinced the committee to legalize the pass, which would become the salvation of a sport that had degenerated into dangerous formations and brutal mass attacks on the ball. Heisman noted, in defense of the pass, that violent scrums based around bruising running plays were "killing the game as well as the players."

Football's decision to legalize the forward pass would become one of the most important developments in football history, turning the attention to the open receivers downfield and creating the pass as an offensive weapon. As important as the legal throw and the catch became, we all know that without the receiver there cannot be a successful pass play.

All throughout Scripture we see successful "pass plays"—accounts of famous biblical characters passing the baton and advancing the kingdom of God. One of my favor-

FAST FACT:

The first forward pass occurred in 1895 when a kicker, trying to avoid a blocked punt by onrushing linemen, tossed the ball ahead to a teammate, who caught the ball and ran for a touchdown. Heisman was scouting the game and saw the play.

ite examples is the way Moses passed his authority to Joshua, despite the seeming disappointment of not being able to deliver the Israelites into the Promised Land. In Numbers 27:12–23 we see Moses obeying God and commissioning Joshua as the next leader.

Passing forward can be a difficult thing, especially when you're used to having the ball in your hands. For the first few years after the forward pass was legalized in the game of football, it was rarely used. But once it was, the game was changed.

Is it time for you to make a forward pass in your life—encouraging someone else to take up the work of God's kingdom?

—MOLLY RAMSEYER

POINT AFTER

In what relationships do you need to retire and let others carry the ball? Are you intentional at developing your receivers?

From the Playbook: Read Exodus 17:8–16. What does this passage tell you about Moses' style of leadership?

TOP 100 Linebackers

NO. 8. PETER BOULWARE   1997–2005 Baltimore; 1997, Defensive Player of the Year; 4 Pro Bowls; 70 career sacks.

FAITH QUOTE: *"The thing that has helped me is to have other Christians, other believers, to keep me accountable."*

79. SACKING THE SACK DANCE

Scrimmage Line:
Designating praise that should
go to God—not us

*"Everyone who exalts himself will be humbled,
and he who humbles himself will be exalted."*

LUKE 14:11

Mark Gastineau generally gets credit for the invention of the Sack Dance. The colorful New York Jets defensive end of an earlier era pretty much staged his own production of *Cats* each time he got to the quarterback, turning a ripple of self-congratulatory celebrations into a tidal wave of "look-at-me" shenanigans. Despite an NFL rules change that sacked the Sack Dance in 1984 (the Gastineau Rule), players still focus the spotlight on themselves when they make a big play—especially when they score a touchdown. These me-first players use methods such as a gladiatorial flexing of the biceps or a slam dunk over the crossbars to remind us who did the big deed. Ours, it seems, is a culture that applauds self-glorification.

FAST FACT:

Mark Gastineau's NFL-record 22 sacks in 1984 stood for 17 years until Michael Strahan recorded 22.5 sacks in 2001.

What does God say about arrogance? In the ancient prophecy of Habakkuk, the Lord promised to use the Babylonians (modern Iraq) as a tool for judging Judah for its rampant injustice. But the violent, selfish characteristics of Babylon positively reeked of godless arrogance. "They are a law to themselves and promote their own honor," the Lord told Habakkuk (1:7). He called them "guilty men, whose own strength is their god" (v. 11). So

God promised to judge the Babylonians too (2:6–17). And we know what kind of trouble Nebuchadnezzar of Babylon got into because of his pride (Daniel 4).

That phrase, "whose own strength is their god," seems emblematic of our day. It's a danger we all face, not just gridiron heroes. But it's a trend that we as Jesus-followers are wise to shun.

Genuine celebrations with teammates, friends, and co-workers are fine. But beware of acting as if your own strength, talents, and resources earned you that success. Sack the Sack Dance in your life. Praise and honor your heavenly Father, the true Source of all our real successes.

—Tim Gustafson

POINT AFTER

What did Jesus say about the dangers of seeking prominence? (See Luke 14:7–11.) How did Jesus view "spiritual showing-off"? (See Matthew 6:1–6.)

From the Playbook: Read Habakkuk 1:5–11.

NO. 9. JEFF SIEMON 1972–1982 Minnesota; 4 Pro Bowls.

FAITH QUOTE: *"I am so blessed by God to be able to say that next to my faith in Christ, my family is the joy of my life."*

80. A LONG TIME TO GET THERE

Scrimmage Line:
Practicing perseverance

"By persevering produce a crop."
LUKE 8:15

When the Indianapolis Colts won the Super Bowl in 2007, most of the good feelings that were generated revolved around these facts: Finally, after nine years in the NFL as a starting quarterback and after eleven years as a head coach, Peyton Manning and Tony Dungy busted out and won their first Super Bowl rings. What many people didn't notice in focusing on Manning and Dungy was that Colts president Bill Polian waited longer to get his first championship ring than both Manning and Dungy combined.

FAST FACT:
Bill Polian has won the NFL's Executive of the Year award six times.

In 1985, Bill Polian became the general manager of the Buffalo Bills. Over the next several years, he built the Bills into a perennial playoff contending team that made it to the Super Bowl four years in a row. However, they were never were able to pull out a win in the Big Game.

After leaving the Bills, Polian became the GM of the expansion Carolina Panthers. In only their second season, the Panthers reached the 1996 NFC championship game, but they lost 30-13 to the eventual Super Bowl champions, the Green Bay Packers.

In 1997, Polian became the president and GM of the Indianapolis Colts. In 1998 he chose Peyton Manning with the first pick of the draft and eventually hired Tony Dungy as head coach in 2002. It was quite a journey, but Polian's resolve paid off big-time.

His perseverance reminds me of the parable of the sower Jesus told in Luke 8:1–15. Jesus said that "by persevering," those with a "noble and good heart" would produce a crop that is "hundred times more" than what they planted. And in 2 Peter 1:6, the apostle reminds us that perseverance leads to godliness.

Perseverance pays off big-time—*especially* when you're doing work for the kingdom of God.

—JEFF OLSON

POINT AFTER

Where do you need a dose of perseverance in your life?

From the Playbook: Read 2 Peter 1:3–8.

NO. 10. SHELTON QUARLES   1997–2006 Tampa Bay; 1 Pro Bowl.

FAITH QUOTE: *"It's hard to play the game of football without faith. You go through a lot, and you have to rely on your faith to get you through the tough times.*

81. THE RIGHT TARGET

Scrimmage Line:
Focusing on Jesus alone

"Endure hardship with us like a good soldier of Christ Jesus."
2 TIMOTHY 2:3

As an offensive lineman during my years playing for the Cincinnati Bengals, I was tasked with protecting my quarterback as he threw the ball. To do this well, I picked what we called a "target" on the pass rusher's body. At the snap, my eyes quickly found the inside part of the number on his jersey and never left it. Whichever way that "target" went, my opponent went. He could head-fake, he could wave his hands and arms, he could give me a leg and take it away, but as long as I locked onto my spot, I knew I could follow it and I would be in good position to block him. With that strategy firmly locked into my thinking, I could win the battle much more often than not.

FAST FACT:
Ken Moyer is associated with the sports ministry Athletes in Action, which is based in Xenia, Ohio.

The Christian life requires a somewhat similar focus. Paul exhorts Timothy to keep his focus by comparing his walk with a soldier's duties. He knew Timothy would feel many different pulls on his time and attention. If he allowed these distractions to keep him from the central work to which God had called him, Paul knew that Timothy would fail.

We face the same possibility today. The things that constantly pull at us can weaken our ability to win the battles God calls us to. Television, the Internet, the allure of riches, the pursuit of pleasure, all these things and others can choke us and render us unfruitful. During times when we feel pulled too thin, we need to "fix our eyes on Jesus" (Hebrews 12:2). When we intently focus on the Savior alone, our distractions will fade into the background. Our "target" will lead our lives, and we will find ourselves in great position to win whatever battles God brings us.

Are your eyes on the target? Are they fixed on Jesus?

—KEN MOYER

POINT AFTER

Name three distractions that are keeping you from focusing on Jesus. Then make it a point first thing tomorrow to wake up and "fix your eyes on Jesus" all day. Create a reminder to help yourself not get sidetracked.

From the Playbook: Read Hebrews 12:1–12.

TOP 100
Defensive Backs, Safeties

NO. 1. DARRELL GREEN 1983–2002 Washington; 1996, NFL Man of the Year; 1996, Bart Starr Award; 7 Pro Bowls; 2008, Inducted into HOF.

FAITH QUOTE: *"I know what my motivation is—that I decrease and Christ be glorified."*

82. WHAT ARE YOU GOING TO DO?

Scrimmage Line:
Getting rid of grudges

"How many times shall I forgive my brother when he sins against me?"

MATTHEW 18:21

On January 8, 2007, the 2006–2007 college football season came to an end when the Florida Gators beat the Ohio State Buckeyes 41-14 in the Fiesta Bowl. Earlier that season, something else came to an end—a long-standing grudge between The Citadel and former player Marc Buoniconti.

That story began on October 26, 1985, when Citadel linebackers Buoniconti and Joel Thompson blew through East Tennessee State blocking to stop a third-and-one sweep. When the 19-year-old Buoniconti collided with the ball carrier, he would say later, he knew instantly he was paralyzed. His spinal cord was crushed, and he nearly died on the field.

Unfortunately, in the years to come, the relationship between the cadet and the military school was damaged as well. The Citadel denied the catastrophic injury insurance benefits for which Marc's father, Nick, applied. The Buonicontis then filed a nearly $23 million lawsuit against the school, its coaches, its team doctor, and trainer. The trial dug a deep divide between the two sides.

FAST FACT:
The Buonicontis helped found The Miami Project to Cure Paralysis, which has raised over $200 million. It is the world's most comprehensive spinal cord injury research center, and Marc Buoniconti is its president.

But in 2006, Marc's old teammate Joel Thompson interceded in an attempt to close the gap. He encouraged the school he loves and the former teammate he loves to love one another again.

On September 30, 2006, The Citadel retired Buoniconti's No. 59 jersey during a halftime ceremony. According to Nick, a pro football Hall of Fame linebacker with the Miami Dolphins, "The Citadel reached out to Marc. You can hold a grudge or go forward. Marc accepted."

"I made some mistakes. They made some mistakes," Marc said. "What are you going to do, take that stuff to your grave?"

Forgiveness. It's a wonderful thing, as Jesus indicated in Matthew 18:22. What are you going to do about the grudges you are harboring?

—BRIAN HETTINGA

POINT AFTER

Holding onto a grudge is like taking poison and hoping the other person dies. Start the process of healing a disagreement today.

From the Playbook: Read a parable Jesus told about the absurdity of Christians refusing to forgive others. The story is in Matthew 18:21–35.

Defensive Backs, Safeties

NO. 2. MEL BLOUNT 1970–1983 Pittsburgh; 1975, Defensive Player of the Year; 1975, Led NFL in interceptions (11); 5 Pro Bowls; 1989, Inducted into HOF.

FAITH QUOTE: *"I always tell young people—I don't care what you accomplish, if you don't have Jesus Christ, none of it will make you happy."*

83. THE RIGHT WAY

*"I seek you with all my heart; do not let
me stray from your commands."*

PSALM 119:10

Jim Marshall saw the ball on the ground and did what came naturally.

The Minnesota Vikings' defensive end—a member of the famous "Purple People Eaters" of the 1960s—scooped up the football and sprinted 66 yards toward the end zone, throwing the ball into the air when he got there. The only problem is that he had run the wrong way, taking the ball into his own end zone, resulting in a San Francisco 49ers' safety rather than a Vikings' touchdown. For this most embarrassing play, Marshall received a letter from Roy "Wrong Way" Riegels telling him "Welcome to the club." (If you don't get that connection, look it up.)

FAST FACT:
Jim Marshall played in 282 consecutive games during his long NFL career from 1960 through 1979.

Don't we all at times do something similar to Marshall's erroneous run? We believe in our hearts that we're doing the right thing while all along we're acting in a way that is opposite of how God would have us to act. Like Marshall did back on that fall day in 1964, we celebrate what we think is a good thing only to learn later that we should have been running in the other direction.

In Psalm 119, we find that God makes it simple for us. If we seek Him with our heart, we will not stray from His commandments (v. 10). And when we feel ourselves moving in the wrong direction, we can turn to God's Word, which he has told us is a lamp for our feet and a light for our path (v. 105). So unlike Marshall, who didn't have anyone to reverse his direction until it was too late, the Holy Spirit is there with us every step of the way to help us walk in the direction we're supposed to go.

—JEFF ARNOLD

POINT AFTER

Ask Jesus to examine the road you're walking and to point out if you need to turn around and walk the other way. It's easy sometimes to go our own way, but often, it's not the path that God has for us. And if we just ask, God is faithful in showing us the way.

From the Playbook: Read Psalm 119:1–16.

 Defensive Backs, Safeties

NO. 3. PAUL KRAUSE 1964–1979 Washington, Minnesota; 1964, Led NFL in interceptions (12); 1975, Led NFL in interception yards (201); 8 Pro Bowls; 1998, Inducted into HOF; Holds career mark for interceptions (81).

FAITH QUOTE: *About a serious head injury with lifelong effects that his wife suffered: "I still don't know why it happened. But I trust that God knows and when I get to heaven, I'll ask Him."*

84. HEART HEROES

"The Lord looks at the heart."
1 SAMUEL 16:7

Each year the NFL draft attracts a great deal of attention from sports fans around the world. Most of the time the drafts go as expected based on months of analysis and computerized predictions. However, there are always a few surprises. Sometimes the surprises are players who are not drafted.

FAST FACT:

During the 2007 regular season, Grant rushed 188 times for 956 yards and 8 TDs. In the 2008 and 2009 seasons, he rushed for more than 1,000 yards each year. He was selected to the 2010 Pro Bowl team.

In 2007, Ryan Grant was such a player. He was a running back from Notre Dame who had not been selected in the 2005 draft. The New York Giants, however, signed him as a free agent, just to see if he was good enough to make their team. They didn't think he was, so in 2007, they traded him to the Green Bay Packers. After spending the first games of the season on the bench, Grant went on to become the Packer's leading rusher that year. By the end of the season, the rushing numbers of this undrafted player paralleled those of NFL superstar LaDainian Tomlinson. In fact, he averaged 5.1 yards per carry as opposed to 4.7 for LT.

How was Grant overlooked in the draft? What is the missing component in many scouting reports? The answer? Heart.

In the spiritual realm, Gordon McDonald calls this our "private world." In 1 Samuel 16:7, the prophet Samuel stated,

"Man looks at the outward appearance, but the Lord looks at the heart."

As you think about your spiritual fitness as a Christian, make sure priority is placed on "heart work" before outward results. Where does heart work begin? It begins by cultivating our private world with Jesus. Oswald Chambers said, "If you have not been worshiping, when you get into work you will be not only useless yourself, but a tremendous hindrance to those who are associated with you."

How is your heart? Is it strong? Is it connected to the power source—Jesus? Spending time worshiping Him is the best heart exercise you can find.

—ANDREW PROVENCE

POINT AFTER

Block your life responsibilities out of your mind for a moment. Are you sensing a quiet confidence in the consistency of your private world with Jesus?

From the Playbook: Read Luke 10:38–42.

TOP 100 Defensive Backs, Safeties

NO. 4. LEM BARNEY 1967–1977 Detroit; 1967, Led NFL in interception yards (232); 7 Pro Bowls; 1992, Inducted into HOF.

FAITH QUOTE: *"Our faith and trust in God will help guide our boys to be responsible men."*

85. HOLY SWEAT

"Train yourself to be godly"
1 TIMOTHY 4:7

Shortly after my third year in the NFL, a former high school teammate asked me an interesting question. He said, "How can I get into the NFL?" Then came the logic behind his question: "If you can do it, I'm sure I can!"

He no doubt remembered me as the weak, clumsy kid who he started in front of during our days playing football for the Fighting Mules of Bedford High School in Temperance, Michigan. Yet I had changed since then. I had spent thousands of hours in the weight room, strengthening my muscles. I had spent countless days practicing, learning how to block more effectively. And I had run a multitude of miles, developing my quickness and speed. All these enabled me to compete at football's highest level.

FAST FACT:
Ken Moyer, who played for the University of Toledo in college, competed in 71 games for the Cincinnati Bengals between 1989 and 1994.

In order to get the product, it is necessary to go through the process. Similarly, if we want to reach our spiritual potential, we must put in the time and effort to train ourselves to be godly. We have to spend time in God's Word to strengthen our faith. We need to enter into prayer on a regular basis to develop our intimacy with the Father. We increase our self-control by fasting. Humility grows from our serving without any earthly rewards. Giving to God's kingdom work draws our hearts closer to the things of God.

When we do these things, we put ourselves into a position to grow spiritually.

God will use our earthly efforts to grow our spiritual muscles. Without earthly effort, our spiritual muscles will atrophy and eventually become useless. The advice Paul gave to Timothy almost 2,000 years ago still rings true today. If we truly want to be more like Jesus, we have to train ourselves to be more like Jesus! It takes Holy Sweat!

—KEN MOYER

POINT AFTER

When was the last time you broke a sweat spiritually? What are three spiritual exercises you can do to begin to get in shape for Jesus? Need to make a chart?

From the Playbook: Read 1 Timothy 4.

TOP 100 — Defensive Backs, Safeties

NO. 5. AENEAS WILLIAMS 1991–2004 Phoenix/Arizona, St. Louis; 1991, Led NFL in interceptions (9); 1999, Bart Starr Award; 8 Pro Bowls; 55 career interceptions.

FAITH QUOTE: *"My biggest motivation is to please an invisible God who I can see all the time."*

86. FOOTBALL AND INNOCENCE

"I wash my hands in innocence."
PSALM 26:6

If you could go back in time to November 6, 1869, you could catch the first college football game ever played. In the innocent, early days of the game, Rutgers beat Princeton six goals to four (that's right, goals!) in that gridiron classic that was played on the site where Rutgers' fieldhouse now stands in New Brunswick, New Jersey.

FAST FACT:

The next four schools to add football teams (after Princeton and Rutgers) were Columbia, Yale, Harvard, and Stevens Tech. They had all fielded teams by 1875.

Football was played a bit differently back then: 25 players on each side, no officials, field dimensions of 75 yards by 120 yards, and the ball was *round*. Sounds more like soccer, eh?

Another bit of trivia from that first game is that the two teams sat down to dinner *following* the game. Then, a week later the two teams played again (Princeton won 8-0) and—once again—they sat down together and had a bite to eat. During this second feast, speeches were given and songs were sung.

These days you will not find college football teams chowing down together after pounding one another for four quarters. It's too bad. Those first two college games, with the postgame supper and all, represented true pictures of sportsmanship and innocence.

In Psalm 26, David delivers some thoughts on innocence—specifically about coming before God to show Him his integrity and purity. He wrote, "I wash my hands in innocence, and go about your altar, O Lord" (v. 6).

Much like a ritual cleansing before God's ancient altar, David wanted to be cleansed on the inside—to be presented innocent before God. Then he could praise Him loudly with all his being.

Are you lacking the quality of innocence before God today? Is your praise lacking? Turn to Him in genuine repentance—followed by real praise!

—TOM FELTEN

POINT AFTER

Pray to God and ask Him to reveal any sin that has come between you and Him. Be still and wait as God speaks to your heart. Confess your sins to Him and repent of them. End your time by praising Him for His love and forgiveness.

From the Playbook: Read Psalm 26:1–12.

TOP 100 Defensive Backs, Safeties

NO. 6. EUGENE ROBINSON 1985–2000 Seattle, Green Bay, Atlanta, Carolina; 1993, Led NFL in interceptions (9); 3 Pro Bowls; 57 career interceptions.

FAITH QUOTE: *"The Bible tells us to mourn with those who are mourning and rejoice with those who are rejoicing. And that it's all right to go through tough stuff."*

87. IRRELEVANT?

"For great is the Lord and most worthy of praise."
1 CHRONICLES 16:25

Imagine having a parade thrown in your honor and having lavish gifts given to you—not for winning a championship but for finishing dead last.

It's the kind of treatment Ramzee Robinson received in 2007 when he was recognized as the NFL Draft's annual Mr. Irrelevant. He earned the dubious distinction after the Detroit Lions selected him with the final (255th) pick of the draft. Not long after being drafted, Robinson was flown to Newport Beach, California, where he was the guest of honor at Mr. Irrelevant Week, which included a parade and all sorts of festivities celebrating his achievement of being the last player picked. Robinson played for two seasons for the Lions before moving on to Philadelphia and Cleveland.

It's whimsical to speak of a football player being Mr. Irrelevant, but it's not so funny if we resort to putting God into an irrelevant place in our lives. We do that when we choose not to spend the time we should with God. Perhaps we pile so many things on top of the time we should set aside to delve into God's Word and spend time talking to God that the Lord becomes our final pick of the day.

FAST FACT:
In 1994, Marty Moore became the first Mr. Irrelevant to play in the Super Bowl. The 2009 Mr. Irrelevant, Ryan Succop, set a rookie kicking record for the Kansas City Chiefs.

In 1 Chronicles 16, we are taught to praise God for all He has done, and we are told to "proclaim his salvation day after day" (v. 23) and "declare his glory among the nations" (v. 24). God is great and deserves all of our praise and admiration. He deserves all of our focus and dedication.

If Robinson gets as much attention as he did for being the last guy picked, how infinitely more deserving is God of our attention for all He does for us.

—JEFF ARNOLD

POINT AFTER

When you look at all you've got to do today, why don't you choose to move God to the top of your list? Make Him your top priority, and set aside times during your day when you can take a minute or two just to spend with Him.

From the Playbook: Read 1 Chronicles 16.

TOP 100 Defensive Backs, Safeties

NO. 7. BRIAN DAWKINS 1996–2009 Philadelphia, Denver; 8 Pro Bowls; 36 career interceptions.

FAITH QUOTE: *"We need to do what God put us on this earth to do for our families."*

88. PERFECTION

"For all have sinned and fall short of the glory of God."

ROMANS 3:23

The 1972 Miami Dolphins are the only team in the history of the NFL to go undefeated and win the Super Bowl. That is quite an accomplishment! Each year it seems that a team will make a run at going undefeated but somewhere along the way that squad will eventually lose a game. Then the 1972 Dolphin alumni get together and celebrate.

FAST FACT:
The 1985 Chicago Bears went 15-1 and won the Super Bowl; their only loss was to the Miami Dolphins.

The 2007 New England Patriots came the closest when they won all their regular season games, marched through the playoffs, but lost in Super Bowl XLII to the New York Giants. And more recently, teams such as Indianapolis and New Orleans made it through most of the season unscathed, but couldn't match the Dolphins' record.

Perfection is hard in our inner life as well. It seems that as we strive for perfection in our spiritual walk, we no doubt will fail. At that time there is someone, Satan, who is cheering our failure and rubbing it in (1 Peter 5:8). That is why we need to be reminded from God's Word of the truth:

1. Nothing can separate us from God's love (Romans 8:38–39). Although we feel defeated and beat up, we need to *know* that God still loves us and longs for us to walk in victory again.

2. God is faithful to forgive us of our sin (1 John 1:9). God is and has always been true to His Word. The Bible teaches us that He will forgive us!

3. God knew that we could not be perfect, and that is why Jesus came to die (Hebrews 10:9–10).

Look at it like this: Since the beginning of humankind only one person who has walked on this earth has been perfect and never sinned—that was Jesus. We can celebrate the fact that He alone is worthy to be our Savior.

—CHRIS LANE

POINT AFTER

Are you a defeated Christian walking with your head down because Satan is lying to you? Confess your sins to God and begin to walk in victory!

From the Playbook: Read Romans 6.

Defensive Backs, Safeties

NO. 8. DEION SANDERS 1989–2005 Atlanta, San Francisco, Dallas, Washington, Baltimore; 1994, Defensive Player of the Year; 1992, Led NFL in kick return yards (1,067); 8 Pro Bowls; 19 career non-offensive TDs (first overall).

FAITH QUOTE: *"Before Christ, I had all the material comforts, money, and fame, but I had no peace. When I trusted Christ, I found what I had been missing."*

89. POST-IT NOTE REMINDERS

*"Do not forget to do good and to share with others,
for with such sacrifices God is pleased."*

HEBREWS 13:16

The job of coaches is like a Post-It note. Their foremost function is to serve as reminders to those around them—reminders of what they want them to do; a reminder of what their aim is; a reminder of what is important.

For each player that reminder has to be packaged differently. Therefore, coaches are left with the difficult task of learning what reminds or motivates each player. Pregame rituals, halftime speeches, individual attention, visualizing the goal—these are all attempts toward reminding each player of his or her purpose. All game long the job of the coach is to correct and motivate the players.

FAST FACT:
Bear Bryant, who won 323 games, retired in 1982 and died in early 1983—less than a month after his last game.

Bear Bryant, the legendary football coach of Alabama's Crimson Tide, commented on how he motivated his team. "I'm just a plowhand from Arkansas, but I have learned how to hold a team together; how to lift some men up, how to calm others down, until finally they've got one heartbeat together—a team. There are just three things I'd ever say: If anything goes bad, I did it. If anything goes semi-good, then we did it. If anything goes real good, then you did it."

Athletes are not the only ones who need to be motivated. As Christians, we lack motivation just as often. We forget what we want to do; we forget what is important; we forget what our aim is.

We need reminders.

What motivates you? Is it correction or encouragement? Have you momentarily forgotten what the goal is? The apostle Paul is like our Post-It note, reminding us not to "become weary in doing good, for at the proper time we will reap a harvest if we do not give up" (Galatians 6:9). That's a great motivation!

—MOLLY RAMSEYER

POINT AFTER

Make a list of areas in which you feel unmotivated. Set tangible goals on how you will begin to make these things a part of your daily routine.

From the Playbook: Read Hebrews 12:1–11: God's reminder to us to stay the course!

TOP 100 — Defensive Backs, Safeties

NO. 9. TROY VINCENT 1991–2006 Miami, Philadelphia, Buffalo, Washington; 1999, Led NFL in interceptions (7); 2002, NFL Man of the Year; 2004, Bart Starr Award; 5 Pro Bowls; 47 career interceptions.

FAITH QUOTE: *"It doesn't matter who you are; God has a purpose for your life."*

90. HAND OUT HELP

*"I will bless you; I will make your name great,
and you will be a blessing."*

GENESIS 12:2

While many pro athletes have become infamous for their off-the-field activities, some have used their blessings to bless others. One such athlete is Warrick Dunn. Blessed with an uncanny ability to elude defenders, run between the tackles, and catch the ball out of the backfield, Dunn landed with the Tampa Bay Buccaneers in 1997.

FAST FACT:

In March 2010, the NFL approved Dunn as a minority owner of the Atlanta Falcons.

He became the Offensive Rookie of the Year, went to a Pro Bowl, and led the Buccaneers to the playoffs for the first time in almost 20 years.

But more important for single mothers in the greater Tampa Bay area, he started the Homes for the Holidays program. Growing up without a father and suffering through the murder of his mother, Dunn was moved to bless those less fortunate. Thanks to Dunn's efforts and his own money, many urban poor single mothers have become homeowners. But his efforts did not stop in Tampa. In 2002, Dunn signed as a free agent with the Atlanta Falcons. As a result, needy women in the Atlanta area have benefited from Dunn's generous spirit as well. Dunn also set up his charity in Tallahassee and Baton Rouge.

So why do that? Why give so much for others? When God called Abraham and blessed him, He explained exactly why He did it: So all the families of the earth would be blessed through him (Genesis 12:3). Never should we think selfishly of blessings received without thinking of opportunities to bless others.

While few of us will ever make NFL-type money, we nonetheless have a wonderful opportunity to bless others. Whether watching football with unbelieving neighbors or sharing the gospel with teammates (whom you would otherwise not know), don't forget to hand out the blessings to others.

—GEOFF HENDERSON

POINT AFTER

Next time you get ready to watch a football game, invite an unbelieving friend to watch it with you. This will help build the relationship and win the right to be heard.

From the Playbook: Read Genesis 12:1–3. Understand that this blessing has come to us through Jesus, for through Him we become descendants of Abraham (Galatians 3:26) and are included in this blessing. If we are included in this blessing, then we must in turn bless others.

TOP 100 Defensive Backs, Safeties

NO. 10. GILL BYRD 1983–1992 San Diego; 1984, Longest defensive interception (99 yards); 2 Pro Bowls; 1992, Bart Starr Award; 42 career interceptions.

FAITH QUOTE: *"I think a lot of guys watch my life. They know that Jesus is real to me and that I'm not going to compromise."*

91. POWERING UP

"Those who hope in the Lord will renew their strength."

ISAIAH 40:31

Kellen Winslow draped his arms around his teammates, struggling to get off the field. After battling heat exhaustion and dehydration through much of an AFC divisional playoff game after the 1981 season, the San Diego Chargers' tight end had nothing left. In a 41-38 overtime win over the Miami Dolphins, Winslow had left everything on the field after making 13 catches for 166 yards and blocking a last-second field goal that forced the extra session.

FAST FACT:
Kellen Winslow (541 NFL passes, 6,741 yards, 45 TDs) is enshrined in both the pro and college football halls of fame.

As physically strong and well-conditioned as Winslow was, the future Hall of Famer simply had nothing left.

Ever feel that way? Are there times when life takes everything you've got, and it seems as if there's no way you can take any more? We all go through it. But we have help. God is there to restore us.

In Isaiah 40, we find that even the young and strong grow weary, stumble, and fall. But here's the promise from God: If we put our trust in the Lord, He will renew our strength (v. 31). But it doesn't stop there. We are told metaphorically that we will soar on wings like eagles, we will run and not grow weary, and we will walk and not be faint. Imagine that: Having a source of unlimited strength. And it's always at our disposal.

But there's a requirement. We must put our full trust in the Lord. Even when we think we're in good enough spiritual shape to handle anything, we must lean on God, who wants to provide us with the strength we need to get through what life throws at us.

Are you ready to power up? "Hope in the Lord."

—JEFF ARNOLD

POINT AFTER

What's draining you right now? Where do you lack strength? Are you seeking the right power source or do you need to examine where your strength is coming from? Maybe it's time to make sure that you are trusting in the Lord for what you need.

From the Playbook: Read Isaiah 40.

TOP 100 NFL Coaches

NO. 1. TOM LANDRY 1960–1988 Dallas; Career record: 418-250; 1990, Inducted into HOF; Super Bowl wins: 2.

FAITH QUOTE: *"Each of us should love God, glorify Him, and enjoy Him forever."*

92. NEXT YEAR

*"I have come that they may have life,
and have it to the full."*

JOHN 10:10

When I was a football player at the University of South Carolina, the popular bumper sticker on campus read, "This IS next year!" This statement reflected the sentiment that year after year, although falling short of a winning season, "next year" would bring better results. It was time, however, for the Gamecocks to win—not just hope to win.

FAST FACT:

In Andrew Provence's first two years at South Carolina, the Gamecocks beat Michigan and went to two bowls: Gator and Hall of Fame.

Dan Stone, in his book *The Rest of the Gospel*, states that some people view the Christian life like an old iron bed: Firm at both ends and sagging in the middle. On one end you trust Christ as Savior and get your sins forgiven. On the other end, one day you will go to heaven. In between, it gets pretty desperate.

In John 10:10 Jesus himself said, "I have come that they may have life, and have it to the full." The Amplified Version says, "I came that they may have and enjoy life, and have it in abundance—to the full, till it overflows." The Christian life is not to be saved for later. It is a life to be enjoyed now—even when we are experiencing our greatest difficulties.

By the way, we did win more games than we lost during my four years as a Gamecock. We enjoyed a few bowl games and even had a Heisman Trophy winner. South Carolina fans continue to hope that the Gamecocks can help make winning an "every year" experience.

As believers, we should refuse to allow Satan to steal, kill, or destroy our joy (read the first half of John 10:10). Do not accept less than the abundant life. Today IS the day. Don't wait till tomorrow to enjoy what Jesus has promised for you today!

—ANDREW PROVENCE

POINT AFTER

What are some of the most common "joy thieves" in your life? What change or decision can you make to increase your enjoyment of God?

For Further Study: Read *Victory Over the Darkness* by Neil Anderson. The youth version of the book is called *Stomping Out the Darkness.*

TOP 100 NFL Coaches

NO. 2. DAN REEVES 1981–2003 Denver, New York Giants, Atlanta; Career record: 357-190.

FAITH QUOTE: *"Because I'm a Christian, I have brothers and sisters in Christ who pray for me, and I know that helps."*

93. KNOW YOUR ENEMY

Scrimmage Line:
Taking a firm stand against Satan's tricks

"Your enemy the devil prowls around like a roaring lion looking for someone to devour."

1 PETER 5:8

It amuses me when people approach us football players and say, "You play games on Sunday. What do you do all week?" They don't understand the meticulous details and the hard work that go into preparation for victory. The physical conditioning is strenuous, and it takes self-discipline. But there's also mental preparation. You have to know your plays, and you have to know your enemy—your opponent.

FAST FACT:

In a career that went from 1995 through 2007, Kyle Brady had 343 receptions for 3,519 yards and 25 touchdowns.

When I was playing in the NFL, it would have been ludicrous for me to go out on the field if I hadn't studied my opponents. You simply cannot just run out there without a ton of preparation to know what the other team might have in mind. The same is true in our Christian lives. If we don't know our enemy, we cannot be victorious.

Who is our enemy? He is Satan. Scripture tells us he is real. First Peter 5:8 says, "Be self-controlled and alert. Your enemy the devil prowls around like a roaring lion looking for someone to devour."

We must take a firm stand against him. The Bible calls Satan a liar—the father of lies—and it tells us he's been lying from the beginning. He lied to Adam and Eve, tricking them into believing they would be like God if they ate the forbidden fruit.

How is Satan lying to us today? One way is by saying there are many ways to God—that worshiping Buddha, Mohammed, and Jesus all lead to the same place. But the Bible says in Acts 4:12, "There is no other name under heaven given to men by which we must be saved." In John 14:6 Jesus said, "I am the way and the truth and the life. No one comes to the Father except through me." Satan strives to blind people to this truth.

So, that's our enemy. We must be prepared to battle him with the truth that comes from our heavenly Father and His Word, the Bible.

—KYLE BRADY

POINT AFTER

What are four things you know about Satan and his lying ways? How can you counter his attacks on your life?

From the Playbook: Read John 8:42–47.

NFL Coaches

NO. 3. MIKE HOLMGREN   1992–2008 Green Bay, Seattle; Career record: 271-161; Super Bowl wins: 1.

FAITH QUOTE: *"My wife and I convenanted together that if winning ever begins to undermine my walk with the Lord, my marriage, or my relationship with my daughters, I would leave football on the line of scrimmage."*

94. A WORD ABOUT FRIENDS

Scrimmage Line:
Choosing your friends with care

"Let not my heart be drawn to what is evil, to take part in wicked deeds with men who are evildoers."

PSALM 141:4

Many freshmen football players entering top college football programs were high school All-Americans. Peter Boulware and Andre Wadsworth, who played for Bobby Bowden at Florida State University in the 1990s, were exceptions. Boulware entered FSU as a low recruit, and Wadsworth as a walk-on.

"With us, people were likely to say, 'If I had to pick somebody to make the NFL, it wouldn't be them,'" Boulware says of himself and his friend Andre. "Even in our own minds, based on our strength and physical abilities, we doubted we could ever play professionally. We surprised a lot of people, including ourselves, when we were selected as the two highest draft picks out of FSU. I was the fourth overall pick in the first round of the 1997 draft; Andre was the third choice in 1998."

Boulware adds, "We believe the reason we were able to improve so drastically as football players is because of our faith in Jesus Christ. Andre and I are both Christians. Our faith is what we've built our lives on and what has given us the courage and strength to overcome

FAST FACT:
After his football career, Boulware became a member of the Florida Board of Education. He also ran for a seat in the Florida House of Representatives and lost by just over 400 votes.

limitations. It has also given us the basis for a solid, lasting friendship."

When the twosome ended up with different NFL teams, Boulware found it essential to have other Christians in his life who encouraged him and challenged him the way Wadsworth had done in college. "I want to learn from people who are living out what they know is right and not just talking about it. These types of friendships helped me stand strong against the harmful temptations that often accompany life in the NFL," he said during his pro football years.

Consider the types of friends you pursue. Do they help you make wise choices?

—ROXANNE ROBBINS

POINT AFTER

Identify two ways you can help your friends make wise choices.

From the Playbook: Read Psalm 141.

NFL Coaches

NO. 4. JOE GIBBS 1981–1992 Washington Redskins; Career record: 248-154; Inducted into HOF; Super Bowl wins: 3.

FAITH QUOTE: *"I'd have to say that the secret to a good marriage is having the right relationship with the Lord and realizing that both of you belong to Him."*

95. WHO'S IN THE SPOTLIGHT?

*"Humble yourselves before the Lord,
and he will lift you up."*

JAMES 4:10

Terrell Owens dashed to the center of Texas Stadium, stood in the middle of the Dallas Cowboys' prized star, and spread his arms apart for all to see.

It wasn't enough that Owens, then with the San Francisco 49ers, had scored a touchdown, he had to celebrate his accomplishment by standing in the center of the field—dancing on top of the logo of the Cowboys—in order to show up America's Team. In fact, T. O. pulled that stunt twice during that September 2000 game.

Neither the Cowboys nor the NFL were happy with that display.

Similarly, God isn't pleased when we choose to put ourselves on display for our accomplishments. It's one thing to find pleasure in the gifts God has given us, but it's another to make ourselves out to be some superstar Christian, trying to look good in the eyes of others.

In James 4, we are given clear instructions about what God is looking for from us. We are to submit ourselves to God and draw closer to Him, and He will draw closer to us.

FAST FACT:

Terrell Owens was selected with the 89th overall pick in the 1996 NFL draft after playing college football at the University of Tennessee at Chattanooga. He also played basketball for the Mocs.

While God desires His children to be close to Him, James teaches us that God opposes the proud but gives grace to the humble (v. 6).

If our actions are to bring praise, that praise should be given to the Lord, who is the giver of the gifts He has bestowed upon us. How cool is it that God desires good things for us? Yet, when they do come our way, it's up to us to live in a manner that points the focus on the Lord, not on us.

Our job is to stay out of the spotlight and give the glory to our wondrous heavenly Father.

—JEFF ARNOLD

POINT AFTER

God has blessed you with special talents and gifts. Rather than becoming prideful in the abilities you have, set some time aside each day to thank God for providing you with talents that bring joy to yourself and others.

From the Playbook: Read James 4.

NO. 5. TONY DUNGY   1996–2008 Tampa Bay, Indianapolis; Career record: 208-139; Super Bowl wins: 1.

FAITH QUOTE: *"God has expectations for you in this business. You're a lamp, and how you carry yourself is important."*

96. MANY PARTS, ONE TEAM!

Scrimmage Line:
Getting along with others in the church

"There is neither Jew nor Greek, . . .
for you are all one in Christ Jesus."
GALATIANS 3:28

One of the biggest challenges of building a winning foot-ball team remains getting 53 unique, gifted individuals to function as a single unit. Submitting their will to the will of the team enables the athletes to perform greater feats than the sum of their own talents would warrant. Starters and backups, lineman and quarterbacks, role players and go-to guys, rookies and veterans: each role is different, but the team needs every one of them. Recognizing this need forces widely varied people into strong relationships. When one member of the team is threatened, the others rise to defend him. When another receives a serious injury, the entire team feels his pain and moves to take care of him.

FAST FACT:

In addition to working with the Cincinnati Bengals as chaplain, Ken Moyer has also led chapel services for the Cincinnati Reds.

The body of Christ is called to the same unity. We can have a much larger impact on individuals and society at large by living up to this singular truth: We all need each other. Some may worship with quiet reverence through time-honored hymns, while others shake the floor praising God with contemporary tunes. You may have a heart for evangelism; others, for discipleship. One may prefer a more emotional relationship versus a more intellectual foundation. No matter where we fall on the broad spectrum that is the church universal, we both need all and are needed by all.

Let us put aside the petty differences that keep us apart, that divide rather than unite. Embrace each other as Christ commands. When one of us hurts, go to his or her aid. Encounter someone with a style unlike yours? Love him or her strongly. See others under attack? Rise to their defense. When we live as the team we truly are, we will see God move in ways we have only dreamed of!

—KEN MOYER

POINT AFTER

What causes you to sometimes not want to help the "team"—others in the body of Christ? Who are two people you need to either reach out and help or apologize to for not helping?

From the Playbook: Read Ephesians 2:11–22.

College Coaches

NO. 1. BOBBY BOWDEN 1959–1962, 1970–2009 Howard, West Virginia, Florida State; Career record: 377-129-4; National championships: 2.

FAITH QUOTE: *"You know what people do? They put everything into taking care of the body. Yet the soul? The part that's gonna live forever—what are they doing about it? Nothing!"*

97. THE WORST LOSS EVER

*"It was because of the Lord's anger
that all this happened."*

2 Kings 24:20

There have been some horrendous losses in sports history, but none more convincing than Cumberland's 222-0 loss to Georgia Tech in 1916. According to legend (which may actually be true), Cumberland had defeated Georgia Tech in baseball 22-0, and the Engineers were not happy about that embarrassment at the hands of the Bulldogs. So, when coach John Heisman (yes, the one after whom the trophy is named) got a chance to get back at Cumberland on the gridiron, he did so. It was the worst college football defeat ever, and the young men of Cumberland had to be devastated.

FAST FACT:
Ironically, the team coached by John "Father of the Forward Pass" Heisman threw no passes in this drubbing of Cumberland. The Engineers ran the ball 40 times for 1,620 yards.

But the sadness of that or any sports loss is nothing compared with the despair that must have swept over the people of Jerusalem in 588 BC when Babylon's army defeated Judah. Led by Nebuchadnezzar, the Babylonians laid siege to the Holy City and left it in shambles. They burned the majestic temple, the palace of the king, and the people's homes. They annihilated the worship center of the people and stole their precious temple implements. And to top it all off, the people were forced into exile in an unfamiliar land hundreds of miles from home. It had to be among the worst defeats in the long, often tragic history of God's people. The loss must have been nearly unbearable.

That's what sin does. That's the price disobedience to God exacts. That's the cost of continued failure to worship God as He should be worshiped.

We may never understand the difficulties of the people of Jerusalem, but we must be sobered to see how much God longs for His people to live in a way that glorifies Him. We must remind ourselves of our duty to live as God wishes us to because of how much it means to Him.

—DAVE BRANON

POINT AFTER

In what areas of your life has sin defeated you? Instead of despairing, what counterattack can you plan?

From the Playbook: Read 2 Kings 25:1–21.

TOP 100 College Coaches

NO. 2. TOM OSBORNE   1973–1997 Nebraska; Career record: 255-49-3; National championships: 3.

FAITH QUOTE: *"Faith and belief in God transcend what other people think about us."*

98. A TIME FOR CHANGE

Scrimmage Line:
Turning change into good

"So Abram left, as the Lord had told him."
GENESIS 12:4

The pace of the April 2008 NFL Draft noticeably picked up speed over previous drafts. Going into that draft, the NFL decided to cut down the time between first-round picks from 15 minutes to 10 minutes. The league also limited teams to a maximum of 7 minutes to make their second-round picks, and it pushed the third round back to the second day of the draft.

FAST FACT:
The year before the NFL changed its format, the fans of the Indianapolis Colts had to wait six hours before finding out who their team's first-round pick would be.

When I heard that these changes were going to take place, all I could say was, "It's about time!" I could never understand why the league hadn't made those changes earlier. Thankfully, the NFL is a sport that isn't afraid to try something new in order to improve. Indeed, the league further tweaked the draft in 2010 when it became a prime-time event on the first and second days—with the third day moved to Saturday morning. For true NFL fans like me, those were great moves!

Sometimes we can get stuck in a rut, and it's hard to make a change. We may keep doing something in the same way merely because that's how we've done it for so long. And yes, there's a place for tradition, but sometimes maintaining the status quo keeps us from something better.

Abram, a.k.a. Abraham, was definitely a man who was willing to make a change. When God called him to leave *everything* that was familiar to him and to follow Him to a place he'd never been to, off he went (Genesis 12:1).

But what if he hadn't gone? Where would the world be today if Abram had held back and stayed put? Thankfully, he didn't.

Change is uncomfortable. We can never be certain of the outcome when we step out into a new direction, but sometimes the real danger is to hold back and stay put. If God is directing change in your life, follow His lead.

—Jeff Olson

POINT AFTER

Is God leading you in a different direction?

For Further Reading: Check out the Discovery Series booklet *Why in the World Am I Here?* at www.discoveryseries.org.

College Coaches

NO. 3. JIM TRESSEL 1986– Youngstown State, Ohio State; Career record: 229-78-2; National championships: 4 (3 I-AA at YSU; I Div. IA at OSU).

FAITH QUOTE: *"My vision is to constantly seek to know what God's will is for my life and follow that."*

99. GODLY INSPIRATION

"Follow my example, as I follow the example of Christ."

1 CORINTHIANS 11:1

All coaches, whether they embrace the responsibility or not, play a role in directing and shaping the lives of the athletes with whom they work. Coaches either build players up or tear them down. They empower or weaken others by their words and the example they set. They create an environment that inspires a person to excel or to fail. Coaches demonstrate how to handle success and how to deal with losses. In short, they set the tone for the team.

FAST FACT:
Josh Bidwell went to Douglas High School in Winston, Oregon. His coach was Rick Taylor. Troy Polamalu also played for Taylor at Douglas High.

Great coaches tap hidden potential and get the best investments on obvious talent. They give their athletes a vision of something larger than themselves and define a mission worth pursuing. They turn doubters into believers. Great coaches are strong leaders, and they inspire great results.

Longtime NFL punter Josh Bidwell has a story that bears this out. "Without a question, my high school coach had the biggest influence on my life from a football perspective. He knew the game and brought out the best in the players. But the biggest factor for me was that he was a strong man of God with a tremendous amount of integrity, which I admired. He never compromised his faith—that was first and foremost in his life. I think that spoke louder than anything. He was available to meet with me one-on-one to talk about my growth as a player, a Christian, and a person."

In 1 Corinthians 11:1 the apostle Paul says, "Follow my example, as I follow the example of Christ." Josh Bidwell found an example in his coach of a man who follows Christ. Who in your life models a consistent Christian walk? Who is someone you admire because he or she follows Christ's example as Paul describes? What can you learn from that person's godly inspiration?

—Roxanne Robbins

POINT AFTER

Write a letter to a person who has influenced you to walk more closely with God because of his or her example. Thank this person and give specific ways he or she has helped you mature in your own faith.

From the Playbook: Read Titus 2.

Top 100 College Coaches

NO. 4. FISHER DEBERRY   1984–2006 Air Force Academy; Career record 169-107-1.

FAITH QUOTE: *"The key question to ask is this: 'Have we honored God with our efforts?'"*

100. DON'T LOOK BACK

> Scrimmage Line:
> Letting go of the past;
> reaching for the future

*"Forgetting what is behind and straining
toward what is ahead."*

PHILIPPIANS 3:13

Playing football in the NFL is a dream that many young athletes have, but few attain. Fulfillment of this dream requires God-given talent, a strong work ethic, passion, and opportunity. In addition, career-ending obstacles lurk at every corner. Injuries, salary-cap cuts, and the aging process end football careers sooner than expected for many players. In fact, while we notice the longevity of stars like Brett Favre or kickers like Jason Hanson, we know that in reality success on the football field is fleeting. Even while playing the game, players understand that the victories are often less fulfilling than the dream. Countless Super Bowl champions have awakened the next morning to ask, "What now?"

FAST FACT:

In 1995, Rich Griffith averaged 15.2 yards per catch as a tight end for the Jacksonville Jaguars.

A relationship with Christ involves passion and dedication as well. However, the prize is very different. It is eternal!

In Philippians 3:13–14, Paul gives us three critical directions. First, he writes, "Forgetting what is behind . . ." Don't dwell on the past. In Christ our sins, failures, and poor performances are forgiven and forgotten.

Next, Paul encourages "straining toward what is ahead." We need to look forward to see what God has planned for our lives here on earth. We can look beyond the persecution, sacrifice, and bad days to the Creator of life.

Finally, Paul urges us to "press on toward the goal to win the prize." That prize is eternity with Christ Jesus. What a glorious future! That victory will provide eternal fulfillment—not a fleeting medal or a short-lived sporting honor.

As believers, we can easily get discouraged because of the difficulties we face. But in the power of Christ, we can forget what is behind, strain toward what is ahead, and press on toward the goal to win the prize. Eternity with Christ is certainly a reward worth striving for!

—RICH GRIFFITH

POINT AFTER

Take some time to think about what is really important in your life. Pray that the Lord will reveal His plans and purposes to you. Then direct your passion and desires to Christ, the true prize.

From the Playbook: Read Philippians 3:12–16.

College Coaches

NO. 5. MARK RICHT   2001–2010 Georgia; Career record: 90-27; SEC championships: 2.

FAITH QUOTE: *"In the grand scheme of things, it is a relationship with the Lord that makes the biggest difference."*

KEY VERSE LIST

FOOTBALL PEOPLE

Brief biographical notes about the football people who contributed articles to Power Up!

KYLE BRADY After a stellar career at Penn State, Kyle Brady was drafted by the New York Jets in the 1995 NFL Draft. For the next 13 seasons, he played tight end for the Jets, the Jacksonville Jaguars, and the New England Patriots. Brady started at tight end for the Patriots in Super Bowl XLII. After his career ended, he took a position as an analyst for the Big Ten Network.

STEVE DEBARDELABEN Since 1975, Steve DeBardelaben has been connected with the University of Miami. He is the chairperson of the University Chaplains Association. He has served as chaplain for Hurricane sports teams as well as working with Miami-area professional sports teams in their chaplaincy programs.

RICH GRIFFITH In the 1990s, Rich Griffith played tight end for the New England Patriots and the Jacksonville Jaguars. After his career in the NFL was over, he became the director of sports and recreation ministries at Woodmen Valley Chapel in Colorado Springs, Colorado.

JON KITNA Despite playing college football at an NAIA school, Jon Kitna carved out a successful career as an NFL quarterback. After graduating from Central Washington University in 1997, Kitna was undrafted by the NFL. He signed on with the Seattle Seahawks as a free agent, and he parlayed that into a long NFL career.

CHRIS LANE Although he didn't play professional sports, Chris Lane can still influence those who do. He is chaplain for the Florida Marlins, representing Baseball Chapel. Lane is also south

Florida executive director of an interdenominational ministry called First Priority, an organization that seeks to reach out to public school kids. First Priority has been able to see Great Commission clubs placed in 116 schools in south Florida.

KEN MOYER After a successful career as an offensive lineman at the University of Toledo, Ken Moyer signed as a free agent with the Cincinnati Bengals in 1989. He played for five seasons with the Bengals, but when his career ended, his association with the team didn't. Working with Athletes in Action, Moyer became the team chaplain, assisting players who need spiritual guidance and helping facilitate chapel services.

ANDREW PROVENCE Former NFLer Andrew Provence is all about character. He is an authorized consultant for an organization that challenges company leaders to model good character at work. It's called Character First! He also is a licensed professional counselor with Good Samaritan Health Center in Atlanta. After playing college ball at South Carolina, where he was an All-American in 1993, Provence spent five seasons with the Atlanta Falcons and three seasons with the Denver Broncos as a defensive lineman.

MATT STOVER When Matt Stover kicked for the Indianapolis Colts in Super Bowl XLIV, he became the oldest player (42 years, 11 days) to appear in a Super Bowl game. Stover was a member of a Super Bowl–winning team in 2001 when the Baltimore Ravens won Super Bowl XXXV. During his career, Stover scored more than 2,000 points, putting him among the Top 5 scorers in league history.

BEN UTECHT When Ben Utecht's NFL career was threatened by a concussion in 2009, he already had a backup plan. Earlier that year, he released his first Christian music recording. Utecht played college football at the University of Minnesota, where he met his wife, Karyn. She made a name for herself as a golfer, playing for the Gophers and appearing on the TV program *The Big*

Break. Ben earned a Super Bowl ring as a member of the Indianapolis Colts in February 2007.

JESSICA WUERFFEL While a freshman at Calvin College in Grand Rapids, Michigan, Jessica Krause took part in a four-hour inner-city mission. From that point on, she knew she would work with city people who need a hand. When she later met and married former Heisman Trophy winner and NFL quarterback Danny Wuerffel, she discovered how that would happen. She and Danny worked with Desire Street Ministries, an outreach in New Orleans. When Hurricane Katrina flooded their home and much of their ministry, they didn't stop caring for the people of the Big Easy. They remain involved in Desire Street Ministries, which cares for the young people of New Orleans.

ADAM YBARRA The first Latino chaplain in the NFL, Adam Ybarra serves the Oakland Raiders. Since 1999, he has provided chapels for team personnel, conducted Bible studies, and become a life-choice guide for many of the Raiders. In addition to his work with the football team, Ybarra has created outreaches such as The Tenacious Group (which helps provide hope and help to young people) and Take a Stand (an event during Super Bowl week that encourages kids to maximize their lives). In 2010, Ybarra started a church, Bridge Point Church in Alameda, California.

POWER UP WRITERS

Brief biographical notes about the writers who contributed articles to Power Up!

JEFF ARNOLD Jeff Arnold once endured an NFL media mini camp as part of his duties covering the Tennessee Titans. When his dream career as an NFL tight end didn't pan out, he returned his focus to reporting. Now a sports reporter with AnnArbor.com, Arnold spends more time around the college game, working as part of AnnArbor.com's Michigan football coverage team, in addition to serving as the site's Michigan hockey beat writer.

ROB BENTZ After working for several years for *Sports Spectrum* magazine and radio right out of college, Rob left RBC Ministries to attend Reformed Theological Seminary in Orlando, where he received a master's degree in ministry. He is now serving as pastor of small groups at Woodmen Valley Chapel in Colorado Springs, Colorado.

DAVE BRANON For 18 years, Dave was managing editor of *Sports Spectrum* magazine. Currently, he is an editor for Discovery House Publishers and RBC Ministries. He is a regular contributing writer for *Our Daily Bread*. Over the years, he has written a number of books for a variety of publishers. His latest book is *Beyond the Valley*, published in 2010 by Discovery House Publishers.

JOSH COOLEY A 17-year sportswriting veteran, Josh works full-time as the children's ministry administrator at his church in Gaithersburg, Maryland. He has written numerous articles for *Sports Spectrum* magazine, including profiles of Tim Tebow, Colt McCoy, Jim Zorn, and Sam Bradford.

DAN DEAL After working as a radio producer and occasional host of *Sports Spectrum* radio at RBC Ministries for several years, Deal left to work on the staff of Ada Bible Church in Ada, Michigan, as director of small group training and resources.

MART DE HAAN Mart is president of RBC Ministries. His grandfather, Dr. M. R. De Haan, founded RBC in 1938. Mart has written several books, including *Been Thinking About*, a publication of Discovery House Publishers.

TOM FELTEN Another former *Sports Spectrum* magazine person, Tom was manager of SS radio and magazine for several years. He now is managing editor of *Our Daily Journey*, one of the devotional guides produced by RBC Ministries. The online version of *ODJ* can be read at www.ourdailyjourney.org.

TIM GUSTAFSON When not serving in the US Navy Reserves, Tim works at RBC Ministries, where the former editor of *Our Daily Bread* currently serves as director of publications. He and his wife, Leisa, have eight children, just a few of whom have inherited Tim's love for the Detroit Tigers. Gustafson has served the Navy overseas in Japan and the Philippines.

GEOFF HENDERSON After graduating from Furman University, Geoff served as a youth director for three years in a nearby city where he discovered his love for writing and a call to full-time ministry. He went to Reformed Theological Seminary in Orlando where he received an M.Div. Geoff oversaw youth, outreach, and community groups at Hope Presbyterian in Bradenton, Florida, for four years. Now he is the assistant pastor overseeing children's and youth ministry at Redeemer Presbyterian in Hurricane, West Virginia.

BRIAN HETTINGA The host and producer of the weekly radio program *Discover the Word,* an outreach of RBC Ministries, Hettinga played small college basketball before trading in his Chuck Taylors for a microphone. Despite the passage of time and a battle with cancer, Brian still has one of the best-looking jump shots around.

JEFF OLSON When he has to put down his fishing gear or his hunting rifle and come inside, Jeff can be coaxed back to his desk at RBC Ministries, where he is a biblical counselor. Olson has written several of the RBC Discovery Series Bible studies booklets. Besides his work with RBC, Olson has a private counseling practice and enjoys speaking at men's retreats.

MOLLY RAMSEYER As a college student, Molly worked with *Sports Spectrum* magazine as an intern. She did such a good job she was later offered the chance to write for the magazine. After college, she began working with Youth for Christ on the local level. Currently, she is national director of camping for Youth for Christ. She lives in Englewood, California, with her husband, Dave.

ROXANNE ROBBINS After hobnobbing with the influential and famous in Washington D.C. for several years in positions relating to public relations, Roxanne left it all behind to go to Uganda to live among kids with nothing. A longtime writer for *Sports Spectrum*, she knows athletes up-close and personal, but she has discovered the importance of the oft neglected little guys and girls who cherish someone who cares for them. While in Africa, Roxanne adopted a little boy named Wasswa.

JENNA SAMPSON While completing a graduate internship in the San Diego Chargers public relations department in 2005, Jenna began freelance writing for various sports magazines. She is currently a columnist for *Sports Spectrum* magazine, and she is passionate about using writing to help athletes share their stories and further the kingdom. She lives in Carlsbad, California.

MIKE SANDROLINI A freelance writer and a die-hard Chicago White Sox fan, Mike has recently had two books published. *All the Good in Sports* is a compilation of positive stories about the good guys in sports. *Bear with Me* is the story of the George Halas family and the Chicago Bears, co-written with Patrick McCaskey. Sandrolini also has written many articles for *Sports Spectrum* magazine.